Ancient Carthage

An Enthralling Guide to the Phoenicians and Carthaginian Civilization

© Copyright 2023 - All rights reserved.

The content contained within this book may not be reproduced, duplicated, or transmitted without direct written permission from the author or the publisher.

Under no circumstances will any blame or legal responsibility be held against the publisher, or author, for any damages, reparation, or monetary loss due to the information contained within this book, either directly or indirectly.

Legal Notice:

This book is copyright protected. It is only for personal use. You cannot amend, distribute, sell, use, quote, or paraphrase any part, or the content within this book, without the consent of the author or publisher.

Disclaimer Notice:

Please note the information contained within this document is for educational and entertainment purposes only. All effort has been executed to present accurate, up-to-date, reliable, and complete information. No warranties of any kind are declared or implied. Readers acknowledge that the author is not engaging in the rendering of legal, financial, medical, or professional advice. The content within this book has been derived from various sources. Please consult a licensed professional before attempting any techniques outlined in this book.

By reading this document, the reader agrees that under no circumstances is the author responsible for any losses, direct or indirect, that are incurred as a result of the use of the information contained within this document, including, but not limited to, errors, omissions, or inaccuracies.

Free limited time bonus

Stop for a moment. We have a free bonus set up for you. The problem is this: we forget 90% of everything that we read after 7 days. Crazy fact, right? Here's the solution: we've created a printable, 1-page pdf summary for this book that you're reading now. All you have to do to get your free pdf summary is to go to the following website:

https://livetolearn.lpages.co/enthrallinghistory/

Once you do, it will be intuitive. Enjoy, and thank you!

Table of Contents

INTRODUCTION 1
CHAPTER ONE: THE PHOENICIANS..3
CHAPTER TWO: FOUNDATION MYTHS SURROUNDING
CARTHAGE..9
CHAPTER THREE: SETTLEMENT AND THE BUILDING OF
CARTHAGE..14
CHAPTER FOUR: EXPANSION, INDEPENDENCE, AND EMPIRE
STATUS...22
CHAPTER FIVE: THE SICILIAN WARS..29
CHAPTER SIX: THE FIRST PUNIC WAR 39
CHAPTER SEVEN: HANNIBAL AD PORTAS ("HANNIBAL IS
AT THE GATES!") 50
CHAPTER EIGHT: CARTHAGO DELENDA EST ("CARTHAGE
MUST BE DESTROYED")..66
CHAPTER NINE: GOVERNMENT AND MILITARY...............................72
CHAPTER TEN: SOCIETY, ECONOMY, AND RELIGION 77
CONCLUSION 85
HERE'S ANOTHER BOOK BY ENTHRALLING HISTORY
THAT YOU MIGHT LIKE..86
FREE LIMITED TIME BONUS 87
WORKS CITED 88

Introduction

In 146 BCE, under the command of Scipio Aemilianus, the Romans completed the utter destruction of one of antiquity's greatest and most powerful cities and empires. The final few holdouts, barricaded in the inner part of the city, set the buildings on fire and threw themselves into the flames. It was a tragic end to a civilization that had once controlled much of the Mediterranean and whose influence and history stretched far from the center of what would one day become the nation of Tunisia in North Africa. The city was called Carthage, and the people were the ancient Carthaginians.

This book will tell the story of the origin, rise, and eventual downfall of Carthage. It is a great story and involves some of the most well-known people and places of the ancient world. The history of Carthage has long been overshadowed by its most famous rival, Rome. And it is through the Romans that much of Carthage's history is known. However, thanks to modern archaeological work and careful study of ancient sources, a fuller picture has emerged. Roman histories often attempt to paint Carthage as destined for failure, always as the perpetual enemy, but Carthage had many successes, great leaders, and a vibrant civilization. It was incredibly important for trade between the eastern and western Mediterranean and was the dominant power of the western Mediterranean up until the end of the 3rd century BCE. In fact, it is hard to imagine Rome becoming what it was without Carthage's empire first blazing the trail of conquests in North Africa, Sicily, the Iberian Peninsula, and even Italy. Would we remember Rome if not for the Carthaginians, a rivalry that spawned the greatest power of ancient Europe, North Africa, and Asia Minor?

The most visible remains of this once-great city are huge walls that were built in the 5th century BCE, which ancient sources claim once surrounded Carthage with a circumference of nineteen miles. We can also see two artificial harbors built sometime in the 3rd century BCE. One harbor housed all of the trade vessels that came to and from this trade center, and the other harbor was for Carthage's mighty navy. Archaeologists continue to excavate extensive burial grounds.

The remains of this metropolis are now silent, lying just north of the Tunisian capital of Tunis. The aged remains of beautiful mosaics bear testament to the once-lavish lives of the citizens who lived in large estates. Terracotta masks indicate the importance of theater and entertainment to the sophisticated populace. They loved music, poetry, commerce, food, wine, and even war when it was called for. They were not unlike their counterparts in Syracuse, Greece, Egypt, and Rome.

What had begun as a trading colony founded by the Phoenicians grew into a mighty empire. But it eventually fell into ruin. During the Roman Empire, Carthage was made an imperial city with a forum and baths; it went on to play an important role in the spread of Christianity in North Africa. Today, however, much of its glory has faded, and history books tend to only mention it in relation to the growth of the Roman Republic, but Carthage was so much more than that.

Chapter One: The Phoenicians

In the waters off the coast of modern-day Lebanon, Syria, and northern Israel live a variety of sea snails known in ancient times as *murex*. These snails produce mucus that was used in the labor-intensive production of a certain kind of purple dye that was prized throughout the ancient world and came to signify wealth and a high rank. The people who lived in this area and extracted the purple dye were called Phoenicians by the ancient Greeks, which signified the color purple or crimson. In the forests of these lands also grew cedar trees. These two products, the purple dye and the cedar timber, became highly sought after in the ancient world.

The Phoenicians developed into fiercely independent and competitive city-states, much like the city-states of Greece. Chief among these cities was Arwad, Byblos, Sidon, and Tyre. We do not know what they called themselves or if they truly thought of themselves as a distinct ethnic group or nation. Early scholarship on the Phoenicians was done in the 17th century, and it was generally believed that their civilization emerged around 3000 BCE and that it lasted, in some form or another, until Alexander the Great conquered the Levant in the 3rd century BCE.

Their power did not go far inland and was instead focused on the sea. They were an early maritime power in the eastern Mediterranean and established trade routes between Asia Minor, Greece, Egypt, and beyond. They established trading colonies around the Mediterranean and are considered the dominant commercial power in the area from the Late Bronze Age to the 9th century BCE. Among their great accomplishments was the founding of a trade colony they called Carthage, which came to be a great empire in its own right. Their trade routes are believed to have fostered the foundations of Western civilization. Their contributions to world history cannot be understated, as they included advancements in trade and seafaring and one of the oldest alphabets in the world.

Did the people of the Levantine coastal cities, whom the Greeks called Phoenicians, consider themselves a distinct ethnic group? Were they, in any way, a unified people with a shared history, language, and culture? They were certainly not a unified kingdom like the people of the upper Nile or Mesopotamia, who were all under the rule of a single pharaoh or king. So, were they more like the Greek city-states, which were independent but shared a type of national identity and shared historical origins? Is it more accurate to say that instead of the Phoenicians founding Carthage, Carthage encouraged the idea of the Phoenicians being a nation for their own gain? The evidence is scarce and unclear.

A distinction must be made between the various faces of Phoenicia, specifically the people, the place, the language, and the culture. The Phoenician language is an extinct Semitic language that was originally spoken by the people around the cities of Tyre and Sidon in modern-day Lebanon. It became a common language spoken in trade around the Mediterranean during the Late Bronze Age and Iron Age. Colonies spoke their own dialects of Phoenician. Punic was the Phoenician dialect spoken in the city of Carthage, which is believed to have been a trading colony founded by people from Tyre. The identification of a Phoenician people, territory, or culture is a little harder to determine.

The Greek sources take us back to the realm of mythology to explain things. One of the earliest mentions of Phoenicia is the tale of Agenor, whose beautiful daughter, Europa, was seduced and kidnapped by Zeus. Some of the sources say Agenor was the king of Phoenicia and lived in the city of Tyre. Europa was picking flowers by the sea shore and Zeus, who always watched mortal women with a lustful eye, decided he wanted to have her for his own. He transformed himself into a majestic bull and persuaded Europa to climb on his back. He then swam out to sea, eventually reaching the island of Crete.

Agenor tasked his sons with locating what had happened to their sister, but it was an impossible task, as they could not discover a secret that Zeus wanted to keep. One son, Cadmus, traveled to mainland Greece and founded the city of Thebes. The sources, however, confuse the story and sometimes say that another son, Phoenix, traveled to the Levant and founded a land he called Phoenicia after himself. Also, the tales sometimes say that Europa was actually the daughter of Phoenix and not Agenor.

While Greek and Roman sources clearly identify Phoenician people as a distinct ethnic group, it seems likely that the people they called Phoenicians did not really see themselves as such. The historical record, specifically stone steles and grave markers, seem to indicate that these people typically identified themselves as belonging to a certain city. Someone would be called a "son of Tyre," for instance, which meant they hailed from that city. Ancient writings speak of fine goods being made by Sidonian craftsmen or fabric woven by Sidonian women. When the Phoenicians are spoken of as an ethnic group, they are usually described in a negative light, as they are depicted as a barbarous, greedy, bloodthirsty, and effeminate group of people. But, of course, these thoughts were written by rivals and enemies and should not be taken as accurate descriptions.

Levantine similarities might not be enough for the people of various cities to consider themselves one nation, but they are nonetheless noteworthy. The Phoenicians were all known for their maritime expertise. The various city-states of the Levant all had similar geographical features: a shoreline to the west and mountains to the east. Thus, it was only natural that they turned to the sea for their livelihood. While Egyptians and the people of Mesopotamia were sailing up and down their respective rivers on flat-bottom boats, the Phoenicians invented curved hulls that allowed them to venture into the sea more easily. The impression is that they were commercially minded from the very beginning. They harvested the sea snails that gave them the famous purple dye and obtained the cedarwood that became so important to

Egypt and eventually the Assyrians.

However, the Phoenicians went beyond this and traveled to islands like Cyprus, Crete, and Kos, where they traded for copper, iron, pottery, and tin. They traded with Greece for olives. In doing so, they also traded cultural ideas. It is believed the Phoenicians gave the Greeks the basis for the Greek alphabet. They took on aspects of other cultures as well. Phoenician art is particularly eclectic and often contains Egyptian and Greek motifs side by side. This has led some to believe that they lacked an artistic style of their own, but careful inspection reveals that they did add their own flair to their art, often adding careful symmetrical details that proclaimed a work as being distinctly Phoenician.

In the realm of belief, the Phoenician religion is much more specific to a city-state. They worshiped Baal, a deity known throughout the Fertile Crescent, especially to the Canaanites. He was a primary god often associated with fertility. However, the Phoenicians in Tyre, for example, worshiped the "Baal of Tyre," who was more commonly known as Melqart and also "Baal of the Rock," which relates to one of the mythical founders of Tyre. One story says that there were two floating rocks off the coast of the Levant and a burning olive tree that had a snake wrapped around its trunk and an eagle in its branches that were not consumed by the flames. Melqart caused the two islands to remain in place as a favor to the mermaid Tyros and founded a city there that he named after her. The spot where the olive tree stood became a shrine to Melqart, who was worshiped in the city for millennia. Similarly, in the city of Byblos, they worshiped "Baalat Gubal," or the Lady of Byblos.

However, Phoenicians also seemed to worship El, the father or king of the gods, who was often seen as being equivalent to Kronos of Greek mythology. El was revered as the ancestor of all the gods in the Phoenician pantheon, regardless of the city-state. But it was the gods directly associated with the city-states that seemed to have had the most attention. Melqart was officially connected to the kings of Tyre and was used as a means of exerting influence on faraway trading colonies that were not directly under the throne's control. While the king acted as a lender and financier of trading journeys and colonial missions, he was also a religious leader, offering divine protection in exchange for obedience. The leaders of trading colonies, called "princes of the sea," who were often the heads of merchant firms or families that had extreme wealth and power, could not be managed in day-to-day affairs by the king. But through religion, they made sacred oaths, ensuring that the princes still acted in good faith.

Regardless of who Phoenicians worshiped, the most important element of their religion was sacrifices. Because of the lack of Phoenician or Punic writings on the topic, we do not know how often or in what context sacrifices were performed. One inscription mentions "the month of the sacrifice of the Sun." But nothing else provides a clearer context. However, it is known that sacrifices took many forms. Animals, food, oil, wine, flowers, incense, statues, and other objects were sacrificed to the gods. The small amount of information that exists about these practices bears a strong resemblance to sacrifices mentioned in the Old Testament of the Bible.

The Phoenicians shared some religious ideas, language, and technological advancements, but they identified chiefly with their cities and family. A prime example of this was the citizens of the city of Tyre. Tyre was not the first Phoenician city to establish trade routes throughout the Mediterranean Sea, but it became one of the best known and possibly went the farthest in search of trade goods. As previously mentioned, the city was supposedly founded by the god Melqart and dated back to the 3rd millennium BCE. Ancient Tyre consisted of two communities. The primary settlement was on an island, which was believed to be impregnable, and was the center of wealth and trade. The secondary settlement was on the mainland and provided the island with water and timber. Tyrian traders ventured far west in pursuit of goods, especially metals like silver and iron. They went as far as Cádiz, a trading colony they founded in the 12th century BCE, in what is today southern Spain, west of the Strait of Gibraltar. The traditional route taken to the Iberian Peninsula was essentially island hopping along the northern section of the Mediterranean, but the route home typically followed the coast of North Africa to the Levant.

For many years, Tyre was a satellite city to the Phoenician city of Sidon, but it broke away and became the dominant Phoenician city under the rule of King Hiram, who is mentioned in the Books of Samuel and Kings in the Hebrew Bible. He is supposed to have ruled from 980 to 947 BCE. According to the Bible, Hiram was a close ally of King David of Israel. Hiram helped to build David's palace in Jerusalem. The Tyrian king continued the close association with David's successor, Solomon, and helped supply materials and workmen to build the First Temple. It was said that Hiram and Solomon established a trade route to a land called Ophir, which was a great source of wealth and made both kings very rich. Speculation is rife on where Ophir actually was located, including theories that it was in Saudi Arabia, India, Sri Lanka, or even the Philippines.

From the writings of Josephus, who is said to be quoting Menander (a Greek dramatist), it is believed that Hiram had to put down a revolt in the city of Utica, a trading colony in North Africa. The Uticans refused to pay their tribute to their mother city, so Hiram had to "reduce them to submission." After Hiram died, the throne passed to his son, Baal-Eser I, who reigned from 946 to 930 BCE. Eight more kings ruled Tyre after this until the crown rested on the head of Mattan I. It is said that Mattan had two children: a son named Pygmalion and a daughter named Dido.

Chapter Two: Foundation Myths Surrounding Carthage

Ruins of Carthage.
Calips, CC BY-SA 3.0 <http://creativecommons.org/licenses/by-sa/3.0/>, via Wikimedia Commons; https://commons.wikimedia.org/wiki/File:Tunisie_Carthage_Ruines_08.JPG

There are several sources that give an account of the founding of Carthage. The main story that survives to this day is that the Tyrian king Mattan I left his kingdom to his son and daughter. The people of Tyre decided they did not like the prospect of co-rulers and put their support behind the son, Pygmalion. The new king's sister, usually Dido but sometimes given the name Elissa, was shocked to discover that the autocratic Pygmalion killed her husband, perhaps in an attempt to find her husband's hidden treasure of gold. Dido then cunningly asked to move into Pygmalion's palace. However, she asked the attendants given to her to throw bags of sand into the ocean. She told these attendants that the bags were filled with her husband's gold and that they must flee with her or face Pygmalion's wrath. They left Tyre and eventually came to a spot in North Africa, where they founded the city of Carthage. Dido ruled as its first queen.

This story is considered a myth or legend and is not the only legendary story concerning the founding of Carthage, though it is the most popular. In Virgil's *Aeneid*, the epic poem concerning the travels of the Trojan Aeneas, the hero stops in Carthage and hears the story of Pygmalion's murderous deed and Dido's flight. In this telling, Dido takes her husband's treasure with her and buys a plot of land in North Africa that is named Byrsa. Some sources claim that *byrsa* means "oxhide." This is a reference to the story that Dido bought enough land that could be covered with an oxhide from the local Berber people. Dido had the oxhide cut into thin strips and was able to claim a whole hill for her new city. However, *byrsa* in Punic (a dialect of Phoenician) means "fortress." This may have been an invention by later writers because *byrsa* is close to *bursa*, which in Greek means "oxhide."

The traditional date for the founding of Carthage is 814 BCE. However, archaeological evidence suggests it was not inhabited for another hundred years after this date. In Phoenician, Carthage means "New Town," and while Pygmalion is recognized as the historical king of Tyre, it is not clear that the story of Dido is anything close to the truth. The most likely explanation is that Carthage was founded, like its neighbor Utica, as a trading colony that was expected to pay tribute to the mother city of Tyre. However, because of Carthage's rivalry with the Greeks and, to a larger extent, the Romans, its founding has taken on a much grander narrative over the millennia.

The city was carefully picked, as it was situated on a triangular peninsula in the Gulf of Tunis with the Lake of Tunis behind it, which provided an abundance of fish and safe anchorage. The peninsula itself consisted of low hills and provided easy access to the sea, as well as protection against some of the wilder storms of the area. It was not far from the Strait of Sicily and provided a natural area from which to control the flow of goods in and out of the western Mediterranean. This indicates that the Tyrians carefully picked the spot for this city, just as they did with other trading colonies in Sardinia, Sicily, and Spain.

According to the legends, after Dido had cunningly obtained Byrsa Hill, the Tyrians dug to build the foundations of the city and unearthed an ox head, which was seen as a sign that the city would be prosperous but always enslaved. So, they moved to a different site, where they dug up the head of a horse, which was seen as a promising omen.

According to the Roman historian Justin, Carthage's growing wealth drew immigrants from neighboring Phoenician colonies and the nearby Berbers. This led to the Berber king, Iarbas, demanding Dido's hand in marriage. Dido was at first reluctant but then agreed to the marriage. She had her attendants build a large fire to burn the memories of her previous life in Tyre but then climbed onto the fire and killed herself so that she could be faithful to her dead husband.

In Virgil's *Aeneid*, Dido offers protection to Aeneas and his followers after they leave Troy following the Trojan War. Dido and Aeneas fall in love. Dido is convinced that they will marry, but the messenger god Mercury appears to Aeneas and tells him he must leave Carthage and continue to Italy. Aeneas leaves, and Dido, distraught with grief, kills herself on a funeral pyre. Aeneas can see the smoke of the pyre from his ship as he leaves, but he doesn't know the source of the smoke. Regardless, he believes it is a bad omen. With her dying breath, Dido asks for vengeance. Since Aeneas goes on to marry the daughter of the Latin king in Italy, with his descendants going on to found the city of Rome, this poetic device allows for the foreshadowing of the eventual wars fought between Rome and Carthage. However, Virgil's poem is not to be taken as historical truth, as he was certainly adding dramatic flair to his verses rather than giving an accurate account of the early days of Carthage.

It seems apparent that Carthage was founded by Tyrian colonists sometime between the 9th and 8th centuries BCE. Carthage was not meant to be a mere trading post but a substantial colony that could be part of the trade route from the Iberian Peninsula in the west to the Levant in the east and as a center for trade for North Africa, Sicily, Sardinia, and Italy. Unlike her neighbor Utica, there is no indication that Carthage revolted against Tyre. Instead, Tyre gradually lost power after the Assyrian domination of Phoenicia and Persia's eventual conquest of the region. Still, Carthaginian leaders sometimes traveled back to the mother city to provide tribute and sacrifices to the temple of Melqart, who continued to be a prominent god in Carthage.

Carthage's location and focus on commerce ensured early success. Based on burial evidence, after only a hundred years, Carthage had a population of close to thirty thousand, while most Phoenician colonies had populations of around one thousand. Pygmalion might have been the Tyrian king who sent colonists to establish the "New City," but there is no evidence to support or deny this proposition. It seems more likely that it was a king from a later generation. However, this would put the founding of Carthage during the Assyrian period, when the kings of Tyre were vassals who paid tribute to the Assyrian Empire. Hypothetically, the Tyrian king who founded Carthage might have been Ithobaal II or Hiram II. This is mere speculation, of course.

We do not even know what the Carthaginians believed was their founding story. Probably the closest source that we have are the writings of Philo of Byblos, who was a Phoenician born in the 1st century CE when Phoenicia was a province of the Roman Empire. Thus, he lived hundreds of years after the height of Phoenicia and the founding of Carthage. Philo's work on the history of Phoenicia is derived from the supposedly earlier work of Sanchuniathon, a Phoenician writer from an uncertain time period before the Trojan War. However, Philo's work seems to be mainly concerned with religion and the idea that the earliest religions were focused on hero worship and the worship of natural elements. There is nothing to shed light on the founding of Carthage.

Thus, it is difficult to say with any certainty when Carthage was founded, who the founders were other than Tyrian citizens, and what stories the Carthaginians told concerning their founding. If Dido/Elissa founded the city as a way to escape her brother, the king of Tyre, then it seems unlikely that Carthage would have had an established relationship with the city of Tyre. It would be more likely that these cities would be at odds. The story of Aeneas is even more likely to be complete fiction in regard to the origins of the rivalry between Rome and Carthage.

Chapter Three: Settlement and the Building of Carthage

We have firmly established that Carthage was a colony established by citizens of the city of Tyre. We know that Carthage was not intended to be a small trading colony but a large city designed to control as much of the trade in the western Mediterranean as possible. To varying degrees of frequency, the leaders of Carthage paid tribute to the city of Tyre and gave gifts to the temple of Melqart, the founder-god of Tyre, who became an important deity to Carthage as well. We know that Carthage's selection was not accidental, as the presence of the city on a peninsula with natural harbors was indicative of Phoenician colonies. Carthage, like other Phoenician cities, was focused on maritime trade, but it also had access to fertile land away from the coast, which helped to feed its growing population. Carthage also benefited from the presence of the Lake of Tunis, which provided fish and a safe harbor. Still, it remains something of a mystery how this colony went from being like many Phoenician colonies around the Mediterranean and the Atlantic to an imperial power and the greatest of all Phoenician cities.

According to the ancient historian Strabo, Tyre founded about three hundred colonies along the African coast. This number might be an exaggeration, but it shows that Carthage must have had many more neighboring colonies than we are aware of. The most well-known contemporary Phoenician colonies of Carthage were Cerro de Villar, Los Toscanos, and La Fonteta in Spain, Sa Caleta in Ibiza, Sulcis in Sardinia, Utica in Tunisia, Motya in Sicily, the island of Malta, and Kition in Cyprus. Carthage was, at first, simply a link in a chain that stretched from Tyre in the Levant to Gadir, modern-day Cádiz, in southwest Spain, where Tyre was able to trade with locals for silver, the most common currency in that part of the world at the time.

At the site of a Phoenician shipwreck near a place called Bajo De La Campana, there was a rocky area off the coast of Spain where ships often ran afoul. One particular ship is of much interest. There is nothing to indicate that it had stopped at Carthage, but given that it was from the 7th century, it might have been on its way there when a hole was torn in its hull. It sank to the bottom of the ocean. Archaeologists have been excavating the site for years and have revealed promising discoveries in the past five years. The ship contained metal, almost a ton of it: tin, copper, and lead from mines in Spain, Sardinia, and Cyprus. Researchers uncovered a vast amount of pottery, the container of choice in ancient times. They had a limestone altar on board, carved by a talented sculptor and perhaps destined for a temple. There were also lead and bronze counterweights, which would be used in the weighing of items to be sold, bought, and shipped. They discovered a wooden comb, amber, and pieces of alabaster. There was also an assortment of perfume bottles, urns, and pitchers. Evidence was found to support the idea that the Phoenicians might have been the first to use pitch to seal their ships. The ship contained incense burners, oil lamps, and fine furniture with bronze legs. There were also elephant tusks and ostrich eggs, proof of a lively trade with North Africa.

Carthage would have been directly involved in the trade of such items. Included on the vessel were votive offerings of elephant tusks with Phoenician religious inscriptions. These tusks should have been in a shrine, but their presence on the ship indicates that the priests of gods like Ashtart (Astarte), a goddess of love and fertility from the Canaanite pantheon, and Eshmun, a Phoenician god of healing who was sacred to the people of Sidon, might have been selling offerings like these instead of dedicating them at their shrines as the worshipers believed they were.

By the time this ship sank, Carthage was a large and bustling city. The citadel of the city had been established on Byrsa Hill, and walls had been built around the end of the peninsula, making it very defensible in the event of a siege. Carthage, like other Phoenician colonies, was primarily focused on trade and acted as a weigh station for ships coming from the west. It was also a port that exported ivory, gold, ostrich eggs, and slaves from Africa. Slavery was a part of the Phoenician society, so it was also a part of Carthage. The Phoenicians were known to buy or capture slaves from Asia Minor and sell them to Egyptians and Greeks. The slave trade in the Mediterranean was already well established by the time Carthage was founded, and slaves came from all corners of the known world and were sent to lands that were foreign to them.

During the Assyrian invasion of Tyre and the city's eventual subjugation, many Tyrian nobles fled their home city and went to the far-off colonies to continue a life free of imperial influence. One of the cities they fled to was Carthage.

The Phoenicians also had a new competition in the eastern Mediterranean in the form of the Greeks. Greeks, who had learned from the Phoenician alphabet and had adopted Phoenician technology in their ships, were now sailing the same waters that had once been used predominantly by the Phoenicians. There were other growing powers as well. The Etruscans in Italy spread their influence, and places like Sicily, which had once been controlled by the Phoenicians, were now up for grabs. The Phoenicians traveled ever onward. There is no doubt they traveled past the Pillars of Hercules, the Strait of Gibraltar, and into the Atlantic. There has been some speculation that they went as far as Britain to get tin and might have sailed down the western coast of Africa. There are even vague suggestions in unverified sources that the Phoenicians knew of a land on the other side of the western sea, though this seems very far-fetched.

Essentially what developed in Carthage after its founding was a new identity. Like many other cities of the time, it became important early on to establish who was a citizen and who was not.

Logic dictated that any important families from Tyre would have been first among the citizens. The exact nature of politics in Carthage is unknown, but since it was a colony, it was certainly modeled after Tyre. However, we do know that Carthage's government was largely an oligarchy and not a monarchy like Tyre. This is perhaps because the king was always in Tyre while his representatives were in the colonies. Aristotle complimented the Carthaginians on their government and said that the oligarchy must have been benevolent because it lasted for so many centuries without a despot taking control or an uprising by the masses.

Like the Roman Republic that came later, Carthage was ruled by two magistrates, which were called *suffetes*. Below this was a senate of twenty-eight members, possibly drawn from a larger body of three hundred. This senate could declare war, levy troops, and appoint generals. Eventually, it would come to be the most powerful branch of the Carthaginian government.

A new Phoenician dialect began to develop in Carthage called the Punic language. This name was, of course, not what the Carthaginians called their language; that is, unfortunately, unknown. The Romans called anything related to Carthage Punic. They called the Carthaginians *Poeni*, probably because of their descent from the Phoenicians. So, anything associated with them was *punicus*, which is known to us as Punic.

The language the Carthaginians spoke is long dead, so no one knows exactly what it was like. There are a few examples that survive in the comedy of Plautus called *Poenulus* or *The Little Carthaginian*. Almost all of the Punic writings and inscriptions were destroyed, but vestiges of the language were still spoken as late as the 5th century CE. Because of the loss of so much of the language, there is more speculative than concrete evidence when it comes to what the Punic tongue was like. Some scholars have even suggested that Punic might bear a strong resemblance to Arabic. Others have suggested that the language of Malta is similar to Punic. Apparently, there is a Carthaginian saying on the island of Malta that goes, "The plague needs a piece of silver; give it two, and it will leave you alone."

In the 8th and 7th centuries BCE, Carthage grew into a regional power in its own right. In about 753 BCE, legend has it that a new city was formed in central Italy on the banks of the Tiber River. It was called Rome. It is clear now, thousands of years after the fact, to see these two cities were set on a collision course with each other. But at the time, Carthage was clearly the greater of the two in population, influence, and wealth. If anyone in Carthage was aware of the formation of Rome, they probably took little note. Instead, Carthage was more aware of Rome's neighbors, the Etruscans, and the spread of the Greeks.

By the 6th century BCE, Carthage would have been hearing some unsettling news from its mother city, Tyre. The Neo-Babylonian Empire, sometimes called the Chaldean Empire, would go on to conquer the Assyrians and take control of Phoenicia. In 583 BCE, the Babylonians besieged Tyre. The siege would last for thirteen years and end with a partial Babylonian victory. Tyre most likely had to pay tribute and hand over control of some of the city's power in the Mediterranean. The Babylonians had their own fleet and were known to engage in naval battles, but their strength was obviously not so great as to keep Tyre from receiving supplies for the first thirteen years of the siege. The city kept going. But to what extent this affected Carthage is unknown.

In fact, it might have even helped Carthage, as many Tyrians likely fled their home city and migrated to Carthage. Carthage might also have been sending supplies to Tyre to help its people survive for those thirteen years. It would seem that Carthage had plenty to give the mother city, but we do not know if Carthage was supplying Tyre free of charge. Given the commercial inclinations of the Phoenician people and the fact that Tyre was in no position to demand anything from Carthage, Carthage might have used the situation to its advantage, not in a malicious way necessarily but simply to extend its independence and to benefit the citizens of the growing city.

Carthage separated from the mother city in many ways but most notably in religion. Melqart had been the supreme deity of Tyre, but he was of lesser importance in the Carthaginian pantheon. The chief gods in Carthage were Baal Hammon and Tanit. Baal Hammon, whose name might mean something like "Lord of the Furnaces," was a powerful god who commanded extreme devotion. His consort, Tanit, was just as important as him. Her symbol of an outstretched figure is seen wherever Carthage left an imprint.

A stone monument with the symbol for the goddess Tanit.
https://commons.wikimedia.org/wiki/File:Karthago_Tophet.JPG

Baal Hammon's symbol is that of the crescent moon. To appease the god, the nobles of Carthage were required to offer sacrifices. Greek sources claim that the Carthaginians practiced child sacrifice. This was long considered Greek slander of an enemy until the discovery of a Carthaginian tophet.

A tophet is the location where child sacrifices might have been performed and where the remains of the sacrifices are interred. The Carthage tophet shows signs that it was in use for hundreds of years. Phoenician cities in the Levant were known to practice child sacrifice, but it seems that long after they had given up the practice, Carthage was still giving children to Baal Hammon.

Archaeological work at a large tophet on the outskirts of Carthage indicates that some of the children were stillborn and that some of the remains were actually animals. However, urns in later centuries held children who were three or four years of age. There are steles that indicate these sacrifices were made in times of great peril and that the sacrificed children came from the highest ranks of Carthaginian society. The inscriptions make a point to explain that the sacrifice was from a noble family and that the child was one of their flesh, not a substitute. The method of sacrifice is not clear, but the Greek sources indicate that the young victims were burned to death, which correlates with the idea of Baal Hammon as the Lord of Furnaces.

It is believed Carthage conducted child sacrifices throughout its entire history. This would seem barbaric to any modern person, but it is important to keep in mind that the Carthaginians truly believed they needed to sacrifice these children to protect their great city. It must have required supernatural resolve to go through with such a horrific act. Just as Abraham in the Bible was prepared to kill his son with his own hands, the Carthaginians were prepared to sacrifice what was most dear to them for the better of their city and its people. Yet, with all of that being said, it is a horrific practice and is hard to set aside as simply part of their culture, just as it is wrong to set aside slavery as just a part of the ancient world. With the benefit of historical hindsight, we know that those sacrifices did not ultimately save Carthage from destruction.

In the fires of Baal Hammon's furnace, Carthage forged a new identity, one that was removed from Tyre. The Carthaginians were prepared to shed the mantle of a colony and become a capital and center of an expanding empire. As the lights of Phoenicia were fading, the Carthaginian sun was blazing against the horizon. This new entity needed land, power, and goods. It would not create itself in the image of its parent, Tyre, but instead in the image of the Assyrians and Babylonians, who had gained control of the Levant. When the Babylonians, under Nebuchadnezzar II, finally won the siege of Tyre after thirteen grueling years, the king of Tyre, Baal II, ruled as a vassal of the Babylonians.

However, this was not what led to the ultimate decline of Phoenician power in the Mediterranean. Instead, it was the decline in the demand for metals like tin, copper, and especially silver. The great Phoenician trade routes that ran from the Levant to the Iberian Peninsula dried up. Many colonies were abandoned. Islands like Sardinia, which had relied so heavily on the mining and sale of metal to hungry markets in the east, were thrown into chaos. The archaeological record shows many cities were not just abandoned but also burned to the ground, indicating there were conflicts between colonies and indigenous people. Fewer and fewer ships began to sail the paths from the Near East to Spain or from Spain to North Africa.

However, Carthage was not hit as badly, probably due to its investments in the trade routes not headed east to west but south to north. Carthage traded a wide variety of goods from North Africa to the northern Mediterranean and back again. Since the Carthaginians were not competing with the Phoenicians, their sudden absence proved to be the opening they needed to expand.

Chapter Four: Expansion, Independence, and Empire Status

The 7th century BCE saw the expansion of Carthage. It was no longer a city but instead encompassed a large area of what is today northern Tunisia. Carthage controlled farmlands, natural resources, and several towns. It traded with the local Berber people and exchanged customs and ideas with them as well. Carthage was becoming the center of the Punic culture, which relied heavily on its Phoenician origins but developed unique characteristics all its own.

Some archaeological remains have been found of some of the small towns within the new Carthage nation. The towns were plotted out in a grid pattern, even if they only had around one thousand inhabitants. The center of every town contained a temple, though which god or gods were worshiped there probably differed from town to town. Temples were often the largest local employers, with full-time and part-time priests, as well as musicians, barbers, singers, and cooks for ritual banquets. Some temples also practiced sacred prostitution. Houses were small and often built around peristyles in the Greek and, later, Roman fashion. The houses often contained built-in ovens for making bread and built-in washbasins in small rooms between the outside door and the living area, indicating that it might have been common to wash before entering the house.

The area around Carthage was renowned for orchards that produced pears, apricots, almonds, pistachios, figs, and pomegranates, which the Romans called Punic apples. The climate of northern Tunisia today is generally mild, with wet winters and hot, dry summers. It was enough in ancient times to support the growing population of Carthage and the surrounding towns. Archaeological research shows that the Carthaginians enjoyed a diverse diet of barley, fish, fruits, nuts, cattle, and much more. The hinterland was also wooded and could provide materials for building ships.

Much of the shipbuilding and maintenance was done in two *cothons* of Carthage. A *cothon* is an artificial harbor constructed near the sea but connected via a manmade channel. These features were commonly associated with Phoenician construction. Carthage had two *cothons*. The first was rectangular and was used by merchant ships. The second was circular and used only for the powerful Carthaginian navy. These manmade harbors were surrounded by docks. The circular *cothon* had an island built in the center where the chief admiral of the navy could stay and review his ships and men.

The exact date for the construction of the *cothons* is unknown, but they would have been a massive endeavor involving thousands of laborers working many long days removing tons of soil, sand, and rock. The harbors had to be deep enough to accommodate the large hulled vessels and large enough to hold hundreds of ships at a time. They are a testament to Carthage's engineering skills. The only visible remains of ancient Carthage today are what is left of the city walls and the remnants of the artificial harbors.

Two Carthaginian expeditions passed the Pillars of Hercules (Strait of Gibraltar) sometime before the 5th century BCE. The first was supposedly conducted by a captain named Himilco, who sailed into the Atlantic and then turned north with a small group of ships, most likely looking for sources of raw materials that were known to exist on the Iberian Peninsula. However, Himilco's fleet went past the peninsula and arrived on the shores of Gaul, modern-day France, after a four-month journey involving harrowing encounters with sea monsters. In Portugal, they met the "Oestriminis," who reportedly had a commercial relationship with neighboring islands for tin and lead. The Carthaginians also visited Britain and Ireland before returning home.

Another expedition, this one of a much larger scale, was led by a man named Hanno and involved sixty-five oared ships with thirty thousand men and women. Many of these were settlers who were deposited along the coast of modern-day Morocco and Mauritania to establish crucial colonies in the area. It seems likely this was the main aim of Hanno's journey, but he continued into the Atlantic and headed south along the western coast of Africa. They went to the Niger Delta, witnessed active volcanoes, and saw a mountain called "Chariot of the Gods," which was most likely Mount Cameroon. In what would one day be Gabon, they encountered hair-covered savages, which were probably chimpanzees. They were unable to capture any males but did get three females; however, they were forced to kill them because of how fiercely they resisted their captors. According to legend, the skins of these females were displayed in the Temple of Tanit in Carthage until the Romans destroyed the city.

In 539 BCE, Cyrus the Great of the Persian Empire attacked and conquered the cities of Phoenicia. Tyre fell to the Persians, and many more Tyrians fled to Carthage and other cities. In the same century, a single family came to dominate Carthaginian politics and gained control of the military. They were known as the Magonids, and they controlled the city and burgeoning empire from the 6th to the 4th century BCE. The first head of this family is typically given the name Mago I. In Greek histories, he is stylized as a king, but Carthage did not have a monarchy. It appears that the power the Magonids enjoyed was allotted by the Council of Elders. Around the same time that Tyre was losing its independence, Mago sent his sons, Hasdrubal and Hamilcar, to Sardinia. Hasdrubal died, but Hamilcar was able to secure the southern half of the island for Carthage.

However, this was not a true conquest but more of an effort to maintain and improve imports from Sardinia, which Carthage relied on for agricultural goods and raw materials. Carthage founded two new towns in Sardinia: Caralis (modern-day Cagliari) and Neapolis. Melqart was worshiped in Sardinia as a cultural import from Tyre, but this became a connection between Carthaginian culture and the new Punic culture of Sardinia. The settlements on the island were largely autonomous, but Carthage became increasingly involved in their affairs and sent settlers from Carthage to the new cities. The settlements became fortified strongholds that controlled the countryside around them.

Sardinia is an excellent example of the various methods Carthage used in expanding the empire. During the 6th and 5th centuries BCE, Punic cities in Sardinia began to flourish thanks in large part to their connections with Carthage. The indigenous population of the island became more isolated and was pushed into mountainous regions. Punic cities in Sardinia began to produce luxury goods like amulets, jewelry, statuettes, perfume burners, and masks, which were then exported around the Mediterranean. Some of the elites of Sardinia were even given honorary Carthaginian citizenship. While the cities were ruled by independent municipal authorities, Carthage still held sway over the island. Supposedly, the Carthaginians had every fruit tree in Sardinia destroyed and banned the planting of anymore because it did not fit with their need for Sardinia to produce grain.

Just as, if not more, important than Sardinia's fertile fields and small gold mines were the Iberian Peninsula's mines. Carthage desired to control the trade of tin out of northwest Spain. Bronze, the primary metal of the age, was made from copper mixed with tin, and no ancient locale provided more tin than Iberia. By establishing trading alliances and founding settlements across southern Iberia and keeping the location of the tin mines secret, Carthage was able to establish a monopoly on the tin being extracted from the area. Carthage used its power and influence to put agreeable leaders in charge of the various people who traded in tin, ensuring that only the city could buy it at a low cost and sell it to the rest of the Mediterranean at whatever price it chose. This practice and Carthage's sometimes heavy-handedness caused some in Iberia to dislike Carthaginian domination. This fact would resurface during the wars with Rome.

For Carthage, however, the control of the tin market made them exceptionally wealthy and powerful. If they could not recruit soldiers and sailors to look into their interests, they were able to pay mercenaries to do the work instead. This was a very common practice in ancient times. In fact, the Carthaginian military between the 6th and 5th centuries grew from a citizen militia into an international military power made up primarily of foreign mercenaries.

It was said that once Cyrus the Great conquered Phoenicia, the Persians became interested in attacking Carthage directly, possibly due to their monopoly on tin and its tight control of the silver market. In order for Persia to attack Carthage, it would need a vast navy to transport the soldiers. However, the Persian navy was almost entirely run by Phoenicians and used Phoenician ships. The Phoenicians refused to participate in any attempt to conquer Carthage, which was originally a Phoenician colony. The Persians were forced to relent and give up on the idea. They then turned their attention to the Greeks, which would start a feud that changed the ancient world.

Carthage's trade networks stretched even farther than their physical presence. From across the Sahara, they obtained salt, gold, animal skins, and peacocks. They developed the auction system to trade with their African neighbors. They traded in amber, silver, and fur with the Celts, Celtiberians, and Gauls. Corsica had silver and gold mines. Malta and the Balearic Islands mass-produced products that were sent to Carthage and then sold in ports all over the Mediterranean. Carthage sold basic supplies to poor communities, often displacing local manufacturers, but they also produced high-quality luxury items that they sold to the Greeks and Etruscans.

According to Aristotle, Carthage also strengthened its foreign colonies by continually sending new settlers. These settlers brought the Punic culture and Punic business practices with them. Carthaginian settlements produced the purple dye and fine luxury goods known throughout the region, and these goods traveled along the trade routes that Carthage controlled. Yet, again according to Aristotle, Carthage sent any malcontents and others who had an issue with the leadership in Carthage to these far-off settlements. This meant that Carthage avoided civil wars and political infighting, which were common among nations at this time. The settlers were given independence and a higher status as citizens of Carthage living in a colony. While this might have undermined some of Carthage's control over her colonies, it proved to be a winning strategy for hundreds of years, as Carthage and her colonies grew.

In 509 BCE, Carthage entered into a treaty with the newest power of central Italy: the Roman Republic. Carthage was already trading with the Etruscans, and the Romans were looking to secure their trading interests. At the same time, Carthage was involved in a struggle with the western Greek powers and wanted a way around the Greek colonies of southern Italy into the rest of the peninsula. The treaty established a friendly relationship between the two cities. No Roman ships could enter the gulf of Carthage unless driven there by storms, and they could only buy what supplies were needed to sail out of the area. Roman merchants could operate in Sardinia and Libya but only under the supervision of a state clerk. Carthage agreed not to attack cities controlled by Rome or build fortresses in Latium. Carthaginians could not stay the night in Latium if they were armed. In Carthaginian Sicily, Romans had the same rights as Carthaginians. This treaty was essentially a promise made by each side not to attack the other directly, leaving Rome open to fighting the Etruscans and Greeks in Italy and leaving Carthage free to fight the Greeks in Sicily and elsewhere in the western Mediterranean.

By that point, the city of Carthage was massive. There were four residential districts that circled Byrsa Hill, a large theater, a marketplace, a necropolis, and large temples to Tanit and Baal Hammon. The aristocrats in the city, who controlled the commercial and military power, lived in vast palaces. There was a middle class of lesser merchants and foreigners who lived in modest but nice houses, and then the bottom class, who lived in apartments and huts outside the city walls. Carthage sat like a huge spider in the middle of a complex web that spun out around it and encapsulated all of the western Mediterranean. Every port and person was influenced by what some historians have referred to as the Carthaginian Empire. However, it is hard to put Carthage in the same category as the imperialistic powers of Assyria, Babylonia, Persia, or Macedonia.

The Carthaginian Empire, if it can be called that, was not uniform. When the Persians conquered a region, they typically put Persian satraps, or governors, in place to deal with any challenge to Persian rule. There would be garrisons of Persian troops stationed in every city under the empire's domain. Centuries later, Alexander the Great would do much the same thing, sometimes founding cities, which he usually named after himself, and populating them with locals and Macedonian and Greek veterans. When the Romans conquered a city, they would almost always introduce massive building programs to make that city look much like every other Roman city, with a forum, amphitheater, and temples to Roman gods. Yet, this was not the method Carthage would use.

Instead, the Carthaginians largely left cities and regions independent but made them dependent on Carthage through alliances and treaties. These cities would deal with Carthage in commercial matters, while Carthage would help in most military matters.

The Carthaginian army, therefore, had to remain highly mobile. A navy was required to protect trading vessels throughout a large patch of the Mediterranean Sea. These were, initially, strengths for Carthage since it did not need to spread itself too thin in an effort to keep every part of its "empire" in order. However, this meant that certain areas could become a weakness if they were threatened by another power or if they wanted to be free of Carthaginian control.

Chapter Five: The Sicilian Wars

In the 6th century BCE, Carthage maintained an alliance with the Etruscans but was ever wary of the actions of the Greeks, who were rapidly colonizing southern Italy and Sicily in what became known as *Magna Graecia* or Greater Greece. The Etruscans were unable to stop the colonizing efforts, and the Greeks eventually settled on the islands of Sardinia and Corsica. A group of Phocaean Greeks, who originally hailed from Anatolia, formed a colony in Massalia in southern France and at Alalia in Corsica.

Things came to a head in 540 BCE at a time when Carthage was conquering much of Sardinia and also dealing with issues with Greek colonists in Sicily. The Phocaeans began to prey on Carthaginian and Etruscan trade ships near Corsica, attacking the ships, taking the cargo, and killing the sailors. Carthage and Etruria sent about 120 ships to stop the Phocaean pirates, who had only 60 ships to defend themselves. All the ships involved in the sea battle were *penteconters*. These ships could be over 100 feet long and have 20, 50, or even 120 oars. The smaller Greek force was able to win the battle but at a high cost, losing almost two-thirds of their own fleet.

With a badly damaged fleet, the Phocaeans, knowing they could not withstand another battle, were forced to leave Corsica. Thus, it was a strategic victory for Carthage, which retained

Sardinia while the Etruscans took control of Corsica. While the Greeks and Carthaginians had had plenty of skirmishes, this was the first large-scale battle and established distrust on both sides. These tensions transferred to the place where Carthaginians and Greeks were already fighting for control: Sicily.

A Spartan prince named Dorieus was born sometime in the 6th century. He was the second born and became unsettled with his lot in life. So, he asked Sparta to support him in an attempt to found a colony in the west. He first tried to settle Libya but was driven out by a local tribe, which had Carthaginian support. He then set his sights on western Sicily, which he was told belonged to the descendants of the hero Hercules. Dorieus believed he was one of those descendants. He founded a colony there named Herakleia. However, the colony was attacked by an indigenous people from Sicily named the Segestaeans, who had help from Carthage. Prince Dorieus was killed in 510 BCE. His elder half-brother, the king of Sparta, died childless, which meant the throne would have passed to Dorieus. But since he died, it instead went to Leonidas I, who is famous for his last stand at Thermopylae in 480 BCE.

The situation in Sicily was more complex than it might first appear. There were essentially four different factions that were, at times, in competition or allied with one another. First, there were the indigenous people of Sicily, who were often allied with another faction, the Carthaginians. The Greeks were in two different groups: the Ionians and the Dorians. These two sides were part of a long-standing rivalry that originated in mainland Greece hundreds of years before when they were separate tribes. The Dorians typically came from the Peloponnese, while the Ionians were from Attica and Asia Minor. In Sicily, these two groups were often in competition with one another. This meant the Greek cities were often fighting each other.

Eventually, however, the Greek cities began to be controlled largely by tyrants who sought to consolidate Greek control of the island. The tyrant Cleander ruled the city of Gela on the southern coast of Sicily, replacing the existing oligarchy. He was murdered and succeeded by his brother, Hippocrates, who began an expansion phase that saw much of southern Sicily fall under his control. He was succeeded by his nephew, Gelon, who moved the capital of the kingdom to Syracuse. Gelon established an army of ten thousand men made up of recruits from Sicily and mainland Greece; he gave all these soldiers Syracusan citizenship. Gelon turned Ionian cities into Dorian ones through his campaigns, using executions and enslavement to ensure that Dorian Greeks gained control over most of the Greek cities in Sicily.

This was especially concerning to Greek cities in southern Italy, which feared Gelon would try to conquer them as well. Anaxilas, the tyrant of Rhegium, encouraged Greek refugees to take the city of Zancle in northeast Sicily. According to some accounts, these refugees were from Anaxilas's home city of Messenia, the island of Samos, or perhaps both. Zancle became the city of Messina (Messana), and Anaxilas was able to gain control of the city. Anaxilas also married the daughter of Terillus, the tyrant of the city of Himera on the central northern coast of Sicily, to secure his position against Gelon. Terillus was also friendly with the Carthaginians, specifically a late 5th-century general named Hamilcar.

At this point, it might be pertinent to note that Carthaginians often used the same names generation after generation; there are countless leaders named Hanno, Hamilcar, Hannibal, Mago, and Hasdrubal. This is not particularly unusual. There are many Romans named Gaius, Marcus, or Scipio, but they usually include additional names or nicknames. Macedonian kings and Egyptian pharaohs are identified with a name and number, such as Philip II or Thutmose III. However, not enough is known about Carthaginian history to give many of these leaders unique identifiers. For instance, the Hanno who sailed to the West African coast is often called Hanno the Navigator, but we do not know if he was a type of "king," naval leader, or simply a sailor of uncommon skill. The Hamilcar that appears to have been allied with Terillus was certainly a military leader, but he also might have served as a kind of king approved by the Council of Elders, as previously explained about the Magonid rulers.

In 480 BCE, Carthage responded to a call for aid from Terillus, the tyrant of Himera, after he was overthrown and deposed by a Dorian tyrant named Theron. This led to the Battle of Himera. Gelon and Theron faced the forces of Hamilcar. Carthage is said to have fielded an army of 300,000, though this is likely an exaggeration. The army of Gelon and Theron was believed to be about fifty thousand. In a small skirmish just outside the city, Hamilcar defeated a body of men under Theron. However, once Gelon arrived, the Carthaginians were defeated in a pitched day-long battle. Once Hamilcar saw that his army had lost, Herodotus tells us that he threw himself into a sacrificial fire near the battlefield. Another account states that Hamilcar was killed by Gelon's archers.

The fallout from the Carthaginian defeat was mild. Himera fell under Gelon's control, and Carthage had to pay two thousand talents of silver and build two temples where the details of the agreement were to be displayed. Even Hamilcar did not suffer a blow to his legacy, which was common for generals who suffered great defeats. He was generally regarded favorably and was honored with sacrifices in some Punic cities, perhaps due to his act of literal self-sacrifice. Carthage was hesitant to return to the island and stayed away from affairs in Sicily for the next seventy years.

Around the same time that Syracuse and Carthage were fighting against one another, the Persians were involved in an attempted invasion of mainland Greece. This invasion was deftly thwarted by the combined efforts of most of the Greek city-states. After Himera, Syracuse tried to present the idea that Carthage was the Persia of the west and that the battle in Sicily was akin to the battles in Greece. The Carthaginians were certainly seen as barbarians by the Greeks simply because they were not Greek. And since the Phoenicians were vassals of Persia, and Carthage was originally a Phoenician colony, it did make a certain amount of sense. However, many disregarded the Syracusan propaganda, including Plato and Aristotle, who believed Carthage represented one of the greatest contemporary governments in the world. Not everyone forgot the fact that Gelon had rejected a plea from Spartan and Athenian envoys to support them in the fight against Persia.

In fact, during the years after Himera, Athens appeared to have increased its trade with Carthage and also requested help from

Carthage in political matters in Sicily. However, Carthage rejected the Athenians' plea. In Carthage, there were some political changes after the Battle of Himera. Hamilcar, being a Magonid, had acted largely in the interests of the Magonids and not necessarily for Carthage. Because of this, it seems that a more republican type of government was instituted. The Council of the Hundred and Four was created. This council of judges oversaw generals and the military to help rein in their independence. The appointments in the Council of the Hundred and Four were for life, and their power increased dramatically over the following centuries. However, after this political shake-up, the Magonids were still in power, indicating that they played a large hand in the reorganization. The Magonids would continue to hold the *suffete* roles as magistrates and generals for many years to come.

By 410 BCE, the Doric-Greek city of Selinus and the Ionian-Greek city of Segesta had become engaged in a bitter rivalry. Selinus defeated the Segesta forces in 416 BCE. Segesta had asked Carthage for help, but Carthage denied its request. It then turned to Athens, which sent an expedition to Sicily that ended in disaster for the Athenians in 413 BCE when they were defeated by a coalition of Sicilian cities, which had help from Sparta. Segesta again asked Carthage for help, and this time, Carthage responded. They were led by Hannibal Mago, who attempted to end matters diplomatically. However, peace could not be reached between Carthage, Segesta, Selinus, and Syracuse. So, Hannibal Mago assembled a large army and took Selinus by force. He then won a decisive victory in the Second Battle of Himera, which restored Carthage's reputation. Hannibal Mago did not press on to Syracuse but returned to Carthage with his spoils of war in 409 BCE.

A Syracusan general named Hermocrates began to attack Punic areas in Sicily and captured Motya and Panormus before being killed in Syracuse in an attempted coup. Hannibal Mago responded by leading another army to Sicily in 406 BCE. This time, though, things didn't go well for the Carthaginians. While laying siege to the city of Akragas, they were hit hard by a bout of the plague. Hannibal Mago succumbed to the illness during the campaign. His successor, named Himilco, took the city of

Akragas, captured several other cities, and repeatedly defeated the forces of Syracuse. However, the plague struck the Carthaginians again, so Himilco agreed to a peace treaty that left him in control of the cities he had captured. This would be the greatest extent of Punic control on the island of Sicily.

By 406 BCE, Dionysius I had been elected supreme commander of Syracuse, thanks in part to his steadfast defense against the Carthaginians in the previous war. Dionysius was first granted six hundred guards after he faked an attack on his life. He was able to extend these guards to one thousand. With this loyal force, made mostly of mercenaries, he proceeded to gain complete control of the city and establish himself as a tyrant. Unlike other Greek tyrants, Dionysius received the blessing of Sparta, which provided him with soldiers from some of its territories. Dionysius would prove to be the model for Greek tyrants and kings, including Alexander the Great. However, as a ruler, he is generally regarded as being the worst kind of tyrant: vindictive, suspicious, and cruel.

In 398 BCE, Dionysius broke the peace treaty with Carthage and laid siege to the city of Motya, which he captured. Himilco responded and recaptured the city and nearby Messina. In 397 BCE, the Carthaginian fleet, under an admiral named Mago, defeated the Greeks in the naval Battle of Catana. Himilco then pressed his advantage and laid siege to Syracuse itself. At first, the siege was successful, but once again, the plague descended on the Carthaginians. The army collapsed in 396 BCE. Forced to withdraw, the Carthaginians lost the cities they had claimed but retained their territories in western Sicily. The island was split between Carthage in the west, Ionian Greeks in the north, and Doric Greeks in the east.

Dionysius regained his strength and sacked Solus in the same year the Carthaginians were ravaged by illness. Carthage did not immediately act because it was dealing with a revolt in its African territories. In 393 BCE, Himilco's successor, Mago II, attacked Messina but was repelled. Mago then led a reinforced army into central Sicily, where he was prepared to meet Dionysius at the Battle of Chrysas. The Sicels, the indigenous people of Sicily, allied with Dionysius and harassed the Carthaginian supply line, causing shortages. The Greeks under Dionysius revolted because he would not fight the Carthaginians directly. Consequently, the "battle" was settled with a peace treaty that gave Dionysius the lands of the Sicels. Carthage retained control of western Sicily.

Dionysius again broke his treaty with the Carthaginians in 383 BCE. Sometime between 378 and 375 BCE, Dionysius defeated Mago II at the Battle of Cabala. The details of the battle are scarce, and the exact location is unknown. It is believed that Mago died during the battle, though. Mago II's son, named Himilco Mago, succeeded his father and renewed the fight with Dionysius, defeating the tyrant in 376 BCE at the Battle of Cronium, close to modern-day Palermo. Dionysius's brother died in the battle. As a result, Dionysius was forced to pay one thousand talents in reparations and let Carthage maintain control of western Sicily.

Dionysius couldn't sit still. He again attacked Punic possessions in 368 BCE. This might have resulted in another drawn-out war in Sicily, except Dionysius I of Syracuse died in 367 BCE. His son, Dionysius II, did not desire to continue the aggression toward Carthaginian territories or allies. So, he settled a peace treaty that kept the spheres of influence roughly the same as they had been.

Dionysius II was completely inexperienced in public affairs and politics, so he leaned on his uncle, Dion, for guidance. Dion invited his teacher, the philosopher Plato, to Syracuse to help reform the government and make Dionysius II a philosopher-king. Dionysius II banished his uncle and ignored Plato's appeals. Dion eventually returned from exile and forced his nephew into his own banishment. Later, Dionysius II returned to Syracuse but was eventually removed by Timoleon, a member of the Corinthian aristocracy who had been sent to Syracuse to save it from despotism and tyranny.

Syracuse had been founded by the Corinthians, which was why the people appealed to Corinth for help against Dionysius II's tyranny. Carthage opposed Timoleon, but he was able to avoid its forces and restore order in Syracuse. Carthage responded by sending a large army, commanded by Asdrubal and Hamilcar, to finally defeat Syracuse and gain control of Sicily. However, Timoleon proved to be able to meet the attack by surprising the Punic forces at the Crimissus River, identified as the modern-day

Freddo River in northwestern Sicily.

In June 339 BCE, Timoleon's forces attacked the Carthaginians while they were crossing the river. It began to rain, which hit the Greeks in the back but the Carthaginians in the face. The Greeks were able to break through the front ranks of the Punic army, which caused the Carthaginians to turn and flee. A few smaller battles happened after Crimissus, which stalled the war. The Carthaginians sued for peace, and Timoleon accepted. Carthage retained its territory on the Lycus River in the southwest of Sicily, while Syracuse was left alone. Many of the Greek tyrants of Sicily fell to Timoleon, and peace was restored in Greek Sicily until Timoleon's death.

It is perhaps important at this point to discuss why Carthage fought so hard to retain a foothold on an island mainly controlled by Greeks and indigenous peoples. The Carthaginians hoped to stop the Greeks, especially the Dorian-Greeks, from expanding their territory and influence farther into the western Mediterranean. Unlike Sardinia, Carthage never used Sicily for agricultural production or to obtain raw materials like metal. Carthage chiefly needed its Sicilian ports. These locations on the western coast of the island were crucial for Carthage to control the north-south trade routes to and from Italy. As long as the Carthaginians had ports on Sicily, they could supply ships that needed to stop along those routes and also keep their navies in those ports to combat piracy, which was always a problem. Some of the cities that Carthage founded in Sicily were heavily protected and had no connection to the rest of the island.

In 332 BCE, Alexander the Great crossed into Asia Minor and was in the process of acquiring a vast but short-lived empire. He laid siege to Carthage's mother city, Tyre, and captured the island city by building a large causeway to bring siege engines against the city walls. Some Carthaginians were there, but Alexander spared them, telling them that Carthage would be next once he conquered Asia. The Carthaginians sent an emissary to Alexander's capital in Babylon to determine when they might expect the Macedonian king to arrive.

The emissary, Hamilcar Rodanus, first claimed to be an exile who wanted to join the Macedonian army. He was supposed to have sent secret messages back to Carthage, but the nature of these messages is unknown, and it is not clear if he was able to determine Alexander's plans. Rodanus returned to Carthage but was executed because the citizens believed he had betrayed them to Alexander. It is not clear whether Alexander truly had designs to conquer Carthage or not. Alexander died in Babylon in 323 BCE, thereby making his true intentions unknowable.

The situation in Sicily was unique for the Carthaginians. They had an army, made mostly of mercenaries, that answered to a general. The general was among the Carthaginian elite, but he had been elected by the Popular Assembly. Still, the supplying of his army had to be approved by the Council of Elders, and he could be audited by the Council of the Hundred and Four. He had considerable autonomy in the field, but his actions could be reviewed by the elite back in Carthage years after he had made his decisions. This made relations between Carthage and Sicily tenuous and complicated for both sides.

A cavalry commander of low-class origins named Agathocles stepped into this theater. He was a tyrant who had gained control of Syracuse after Timoleon's death. Agathocles styled himself as an Alexander for the west and saw Carthage as the western version of Persia. He massacred the oligarchs of Syracuse. Soon, he declared war on the Carthaginians, and they met at the Battle of Himera. The Punic army was led by Hamilcar, grandson of Hanno the Great. Agathocles was defeated at the battle and limped back to Syracuse, where the Carthaginians then laid siege. In a surprise move, he was able to break the blockade in 310 BCE and took an army to North Africa, where he landed on Cape Bon.

He defeated the Carthaginian force there and camped near Tunis. Agathocles began to capture several cities in North Africa. He allied with Ophellas, the ruler of Cyrenaica, and promised Ophellas that he could keep any African possessions they took from Carthage. When Ophellas arrived, Agathocles attacked his army and had Ophellas killed. He took control of what remained of the Cyrenaican army. In 307 BCE, Agathocles was decisively defeated and fled back to Sicily. He concluded a peace treaty with Carthage, which left him in control of several Greek cities on the east side of the island. Carthage maintained control of a portion of its ports in the west.

This peace remained until the appearance of King Pyrrhus of Epirus in Sicily, where he took control of the eastern Greek part. It was said that Pyrrhus had been requested to come there by Greeks living on the island, as they wanted him to deliver them from the Carthaginians. In 297 BCE, the Carthaginians were concerned that Pyrrhus would involve himself in Sicily. Pyrrhus had been in Italy, battling the Romans successfully but at a great cost. This is the origin of the term "Pyrrhic victory." The Carthaginians knew that the Greeks in Sicily were asking for assistance from Pyrrhus, so they sent a commander with 120 ships to Rome to offer help in defeating this potential foe. The Roman Senate declined the offer. However, there is some evidence that Rome and Carthage made another treaty at this time. It is also believed that at some point, the Carthaginians took Roman soldiers from Sicily and transported them to Rhegium to deal with a rebel Roman garrison. The Punic ships then waited to see if Pyrrhus made an attempt to cross to Sicily.

Pyrrhus did so in the late 3rd century BCE. He married Agathocles's daughter after the king of Syracuse died. Pyrrhus quickly attacked Carthaginian possessions, conquering Selinus, Halicyae, Segesta, and other cities. He besieged Eryx and eventually took that city as well. According to Diodorus Siculus, Pyrrhus took every Carthaginian city in Sicily until he was stopped at the last city, Lilybaeum, where the Carthaginians had finally been able to provide troops, grain, and catapults. Around this same time, it appears that the Greeks in Sicily were beginning to tire of Pyrrhus's rule, as he behaved as a despot and was suspicious of those who tried to help him. He received messages asking for his return to Italy, which he took as an excuse to leave. With Pyrrhus's departure, the Carthaginians became interested in regaining their possessions in the western part of Sicily, if not gaining control of the whole island. Unfortunately, their situation would prove to be much more dangerous.

Chapter Six: The First Punic War

Artist depiction of a Carthaginian hoplite.
User:Aldo Ferruggia, CC BY-SA 3.0 <https://creativecommons.org/licenses/by-sa/3.0>, via Wikimedia Commons;
https://commons.wikimedia.org/wiki/File:Carthaginian_hoplite_-_Oplita_cartaginese.JPG

In the 280s BCE, a group of Italian mercenaries called the "Sons of Mars" or Mamertines took control of the strategically important city of Messina in northern Sicily. This city lay just across the Strait of Sicily from Italy and was an excellent base from which to control the flow of ships through the strait and from Sicily to Italy and back. When Pyrrhus was in Sicily, he had been asked to remove the Mamertines but had been either unwilling or unable to comply. After his departure and eventual defeat in Italy, Syracuse appointed Hiero II to be the commander of the city's troops. The Mamertines threatened Syracuse, and Hiero defeated them in battle but was stopped from taking the city of Messina by the Carthaginians. In 264 BCE, he attacked the Mamertines again after he had been declared king of Syracuse.

The Mamertines contacted both the Carthaginians and the Romans for help. By this time, Rome had defeated the Samnites, Etruscans, and the Greek cities of Italy and now controlled the entire peninsula. There is strong evidence to support the idea that Rome and Carthage not only considered each other allies up to this point but had also actively traded with each other. There were Carthaginians living in Rome and in other cities in Italy. Archaeological evidence shows that Rome's "African" district was occupied long before war broke out between the two superpowers.

Rome had certain advantages compared to other western Mediterranean nations. When the Romans conquered a city or land, they not only infused the Roman identity but also required a certain number of soldiers from their new territories. This meant the Roman army was made up largely of citizen soldiers and not mercenaries, which proved beneficial because the troops could be induced to fight for an ideal and not just a paycheck. Also, because of Rome's political structure, with senators and consuls holding office for a short time, it made it very difficult for Rome to sue for peace or work out any treaties with an enemy. No one in Rome had the personal power to surrender. This meant that even after several defeats, such as in their first battles with Pyrrhus, the Romans did not give up but kept fighting because they had no other option. This institutional tenacity would prove to be a hallmark of Rome's fighting prowess. And yet, Carthage was certainly the greater of the two when the Mamertines requested help against Hiero II.

The Carthaginians arrived first, and they may have been contacted first, but the Mamertines' plea to Rome was as fellow Italians. Rome was at first unsure of becoming involved outside of Italy, but it feared what would happen if Carthage had control of Messina. The Romans hoped to take control of Syracuse if they defeated Hiero, though. The Romans sent an army under the command of Appius Claudius Caudex to aid the Mamertines, although they also wished to stop the Carthaginians from gaining any new territories on the island. Upon learning about the approach of the Romans, the Carthaginian general took the fateful step of leaving Messina and allying himself with Hiero. This combined force then besieged Messina (Messana). Rome and Carthage declared war on each other. It was 264 BCE, and the First Punic War had begun.

These opening hostilities were largely possible because Carthage, whose navy was much greater than anything Rome could muster, consistently failed to stop the Romans from crossing into Sicily. At one point, the Romans were even able to take a Punic ship, and they managed several large-scale crossings with mainly borrowed ships from their southern Italian territories. How this was possible remains something of a mystery. The Romans certainly used every trick they could think of to their advantage, but Carthage's navy was highly experienced in patrolling the waters. Luck cannot be completely discounted, of course.

Regardless, Rome's ability to land tens of thousands of troops on the island caused an immediate response. Many cities formed alliances with Rome. Hiero, who was isolated from support, sued for peace. Skirmishes between Romans and Carthaginians broke out, but not much was accomplished, and both sides claimed early victories.

Hiero became a friend and ally to Rome and was able to remain on the throne of Syracuse. The Punic general who had lost Messina to Rome and failed to stop the Romans from crossing over to Sicily was crucified for cowardice. The combined loss of Messina and Syracuse was a devastating blow to Carthage because it meant that Rome had secure ports where they could land troops. While no large battles had yet been fought, Rome had won a great strategic victory. While some might argue that Rome and Carthage had long been on a collision course toward each other, this is not entirely accurate. The truth was more subtle. Carthage had long been a great power in the area, and Rome had now made itself another great power in the same area. They eyed each other suspiciously and with jealousy. They both wanted to acquire more but also feared the loss of what they already had. Both sides saw each other (correctly) as adversaries in a game of empires. If either of them missed an opportunity or gave up an inch of influence, they opened themselves up to domination by the other.

Rome had already begun to identify itself as part of the Greek tradition. The Romans believed they were descended from the Trojan Aeneas, who came to be thought of as Greek even though he had fought against the Greeks in the Trojan War. In fact, the Trojans shared much in common with the Greeks, or at least that is how later writers and historians depicted it. The Romans had also come to accept the cult of Hercules into their religious calendar and believed that Hercules had figured prominently in their past. Some elite Roman families claimed to be descended directly from the great Greek warrior.

Carthage, on the other hand, had come to be associated with the Orient and the East, despite their geographical location. They had come from the Phoenicians, who were certainly not Greeks but instead "barbarians" from the Levant. This cultural divide between the Romans and Carthaginians was magnified in the years before the First Punic War. Therefore, the elites in Rome were already largely convinced of the Carthaginians' treachery and duplicity. Carthage might have felt something similar, but we can't know for sure because no writings from Carthage survived. The Punic culture owed much to the Phoenicians, but it was also largely its own creation and incorporated deities from Iberia and Sardinia, to name just a few. The Carthaginians most likely felt no connection to the Greeks, but their ancestors' stories went back much further. The Phoenicians were sailing the Mediterranean when the Greeks were still unrecognizable tribes. The Carthaginians most likely felt that their pedigree was more than adequate. The Romans were essentially invading foreigners, but the Carthaginians had no real claim to Sicily either. The two would be fighting over an island that wasn't a homeland to either of them. Yet, they each felt that the actions of the other were a legitimate cause for war.

In 262 BCE, Carthage decided to establish a base of operations at Akragas on the southwest side of Sicily. The Carthaginian strategy is not known, but it is clear they were pinning their hopes on their superior navy. Akragas was easily defendable and could be reached by Punic ships with ease. Rome essentially had no navy but instead relied on the ships of allies to transport its substantial land forces. Upon learning that the Carthaginians were in Akragas, the Romans besieged the city. The Carthaginians sent a force to relieve the besieged city. The Punic commander, Hanno, son of Hannibal, took his fifty thousand infantry units, six thousand cavalrymen, and sixty war elephants to Akragas after landing. However, Hanno seems to have had little confidence in his soldiers, as they camped for two months without attacking the Romans.

Finally, he could take it no longer and advanced on the Roman army, putting his elephants behind his soldiers, most likely to keep them from retreating. The Romans were able to push the Carthaginian lines back, and the elephants panicked, trampling on their own men. A considerable number of Carthaginians were lost, and their baggage train was taken. Upon returning to Carthage, Hanno lost his civil rights and had to pay a fine of six thousand gold pieces. The battle he lost was called the Battle of Agrigentum and is considered the first real battle of the Punic Wars.

Plans for a Roman navy began in 260 BCE after the Carthaginians began harassing the Italian coast. The Romans used the Carthaginian quinquereme, which had been captured very early in the war, as their model. Quinqueremes were large warships with three banks of oars, with two men on the top oar, two on the center oar, and one man on the bottom oar. Once the Romans began to build ships in earnest, they were finished in only two months. Rome's new admiral was consul Gnaeus Cornelius Scipio, and like every other Roman aristocrat engaged in military action, he didn't have the luxury to bide his time. He needed to act quickly. Rome's goal was now clear. If it could face and defeat

Carthage's powerful navy, then the Punic presence in Sicily would be gone forever.

After Rome's victory at Agrigentum, it attempted to take other cities controlled by Carthage, but that proved difficult and costly. Cities would be taken by either side, then taken back by the other. Allegiances switched dramatically in a bloody stalemate that proved unsatisfying to both sides. This was why the Senate in Rome felt certain that the only course available to the Romans was with their new navy. They trained the oarsmen relentlessly and took their ships out often to go through various maneuvers so that the sailors' reactions would be automatic with no hesitation. Rome and Carthage ships met in brief skirmishes, with the Romans usually losing to the more experienced Carthaginians.

However, the Romans began to realize they might have the upper hand if they could turn a naval battle into something more like a land battle, which was where their soldiers could do what they did best. With that in mind, they began to implement the use of the *corvus* or "crow," which was a hooked gangplank that could latch onto the side of an enemy ship and allow it to be boarded.

The Roman admiral Scipio led seventeen ships in 260 BCE to the Aeolian Islands, where he was prepared to accept the surrender of the city of Lipara (modern-day Lipari). However, the Carthaginians arrived as well and trapped Scipio in the harbor. The inexperienced Roman crew abandoned their ships and were quickly captured, along with their commander. Scipio was ransomed back to the Romans but was not punished for the loss. He even became consul again in 254 BCE. Scipio was replaced as admiral by Gaius Duilius. It took some time for Duilius to arrive in Sicily, so the Romans made much-needed repairs to their hastily built ships, trained, and worked more with the *corvus*.

When Duilius arrived, he left Sicily in the hands of his lieutenants and led the Roman fleet in a full-scale assault on the Carthaginians. They met each other at Mylae in 260 BCE. The commander of the Carthaginians was Hannibal Gisco, who had been at the Battle of Agrigentum. Gisco saw the Roman fleet of 103 ships and approached them rapidly with his 130 ships. The Carthaginians, it would seem, were overly confident in their prowess at sea. If it had been a typical naval battle, they might have been well founded in their confidence. But the Romans were planning on a much different type of battle. As soon as the Carthaginians came within range, they dropped their "crows," and Roman marines quickly boarded the Carthaginian ships and dispatched everyone on board. According to ancient historians, thirty ships were taken in this way before the Carthaginians knew what was happening, but it was too late for the rest. Their momentum propelled them right into the arms of their destruction.

Gisco was barely able to escape in a rowboat. He was also able to escape punishment back in Carthage by sending a message asking if he should attack the Romans. When Carthage said yes, he claimed he was only following orders. The Romans were now emboldened and pursued Gisco to Sardinia, where they defeated another Carthaginian fleet. This time, Hannibal Gisco was not so lucky and was executed by his own subordinates.

Surprisingly, while the Carthaginian navy was suffering, their land army in Sicily was doing well. The Carthaginians were engaged in a war of attrition in the hilly Sicilian terrain. This did not work well for Roman generals, who wanted decisive action since their consulship only lasted one year. The Carthaginian commanders, who held their positions for much longer, could afford to play a longer game. The Romans would besiege Carthaginian strongholds but would have to give up after several months. Cities continued to switch sides sporadically throughout the conflict. The city of Enna, for example, changed sides three times in five years. Cities like Panormus and Lilybaeum stayed in Carthaginian hands consistently. This still did not counteract their losses at sea. The Romans raided Malta and the Aeolian Islands and scored a victory against the Carthaginians off Cape Tyndaris on the northern coast of Sicily.

The Romans then decided to pursue a familiar course of action. They would take the fight directly to North Africa. This was a daring plan. Before this, the only Roman action outside Italy had been their crossing to Sicily. Now they were planning an invasion almost 373 miles across the open ocean. The Romans put together a fleet of 330 ships, with 120 marines assigned to each vessel and a certain number of oarsmen. The ancient historian Polybius tells us the Romans had a total of 140,000 men. The Carthaginians had an estimated 350 ships and 150,000 men. These massive navies met at Cape Ecnomus off the southern side of Sicily. Once again, the Roman *corvi* proved to be the defining element of the battle. The Carthaginians were laid out in a line, while the Roman ships were broken into four parts, making a triangle, with one section held in reserve.

The Carthaginian center crumbled first. The line collapsed in on itself, and the Romans were able to surround a large portion of the Carthaginian fleet. In all, ninety-four Punic ships were taken or sunk, with the Romans only losing twenty-four. It was a complete disaster for the Carthaginians. Their much smaller fleet regrouped, probably at Lilybaeum. They sent a new commander named Hanno to present peace terms to Rome, which were rejected. One commander, Hamilcar, stayed in Sicily, while Hanno took most of the fleet back to North Africa. The Romans continued on their mission and landed at a place called Aspis on Cape Bon, a peninsula in northern Tunisia, and quickly captured the city.

Rome perhaps second-guessed its decision to send two consuls and such a large army to North Africa, as it recalled one of the consuls, Manlius Vulso, back to Italy. This left the other consul, Marcus Atilius Regulus, with forty ships, fifteen thousand infantry, and five hundred cavalry. Regulus besieged the city of Adys, with the Carthaginians sending five thousand infantry and five hundred cavalry against them.

When the forces met in battle, the Carthaginians pushed the Roman lines back, but upon chasing after the Roman center, they found themselves surrounded. They turned and fled in disarray. Tunis was then taken by Regulus. Carthage was overrun with refugees fleeing the Romans.

Famine began to set in within the great city. Peace negotiations began, but Regulus demanded that the Carthaginians leave Sicily and Sardinia, pay ransoms for every Carthaginian prisoner, pay Rome's war expenses, and pay a yearly tribute. Regulus also demanded that Carthage get Rome's consent for any future declarations of war or peace and that Carthage be left with only one warship. The Carthaginians would never agree to such terms, which Regulus was counting on. He wanted to take Carthage itself and desired the plunder from such a great prize.

Carthage brought in new mercenaries, including a Spartan commander named Xanthippus. Carthage mustered twelve thousand infantry, four thousand cavalry, and one hundred war elephants. Xanthippus was put in charge of the entire force, perhaps showing that Carthage recognized the issue with their homegrown commanders. He attacked the Romans immediately and defeated them, thanks in large part to his superior cavalry. The Roman army was almost totally destroyed or captured; only about two thousand Roman soldiers were able to escape. Regulus was captured and died in captivity. North Africa had been saved. Xanthippus recognized his precarious position and the jealousy directed toward him, so he took his honors for the victory and left Carthage.

Rome still had control of the sea, though. Fortune favored Carthage in this one respect, as the Roman fleet was caught in a storm off the southern coast of Sicily in 255 BCE. Only 80 of 364 ships survived. However, things in Sicily were looking bad for the Carthaginians. The port of Panormus was taken in 254 BCE. Then, Thermae Himerae and Lipara fell in 252 BCE. Akragas was retaken, but the Carthaginian commander knew he couldn't keep it, so he had the city burned to the ground. An attempt was made to retake Panormus, but it was a failure, with twenty thousand Carthaginian troops lost.

Lilybaeum became the next Roman target. In 250 BCE, the Romans laid siege to the city by land and sea. The Carthaginians focused on breaking through the naval blockade with supplies and fresh troops. The hero of these blockade runs was a captain named Hannibal the Rhodian, who entered the harbor of Lilybaeum at least twice and challenged the Romans to battle, which they declined due to his fast and agile ship. However, one of the Punic quadriremes was stopped and captured by the Romans. This ship was then used by the Romans to hunt down Hannibal the Rhodian, whose own ship was captured and used by the Romans to completely seal off the harbor of Lilybaeum.

The constant warfare, the loss of Sicilian ports, and the dominance of the Romans at sea led to economic exhaustion in

Carthage. In 247 BCE, Carthage was reduced to asking for a loan of two thousand talents from Ptolemy in Egypt; the request was quickly denied.

Despite the devastation to Rome's navy in the storm of 255 BCE, Rome had finally been able to rebuild their fleet. Things remained a stalemate in Sicily. The one bright spot for Carthage was the actions of a commander named Hamilcar Barca, who conducted guerilla warfare of a mostly symbolic nature; he was not necessarily concerned with strategic goals. In Carthage, public opinion had shifted to a desire for peace. Rome had simply outlasted Carthage in its desire to continue hostilities. Carthage had never been able to adapt to Rome's highly aggressive strategy or develop a clear strategy of its own. Instead, the Carthaginians had largely been fighting a defensive war. They were not trying to win; they were simply trying not to lose.

The terms of peace that Rome offered were more appealing than the demands that Regulus had made. Carthage would need to surrender all its possessions in Sicily and its naval ports on neighboring islands. The Carthaginians could not be in conflict with Rome or her allies. They were also required to pay 3,200 talents or almost 100 tons of silver.

The war had lasted a grueling twenty-three years. Both sides had lost hundreds of ships and hundreds of thousands of soldiers, many lost at sea. The two sides had started off as wary adversaries with a history of treaties and trade. Now, they were bitter enemies. The Romans would speak of *Punica fides* or "Carthaginian loyalty," which meant the worst sort of betrayal. The peace after the First Punic War would last twenty-three years, but the stage had been set for an even greater war.

In the following years, Carthage's mercenaries and African allies turned against her in the Mercenary War, which lasted from 241 to 237 BCE. Rome nominally supported Carthage in the war but used the opportunity to take Sardinia and Corsica from Carthage. Carthage was able to suppress the rebellion thanks to Hamilcar Barca, who began to show a knack for great leadership. Consequently, his family grew exceptionally powerful. Hamilcar turned his sights on Hispania, modern-day Spain, instead of attempting to retake Sardinia, Corsica, or Sicily back from Rome.

Hispania already had a Punic presence and was known for its excellent natural resources and good ports for expanded trade.

By the 220s BCE, thanks to its new territories in Hispania, Carthage had recovered from its war with Rome. Rome acknowledged Carthage's expansion in Spain and focused on governing her new burgeoning empire. From 225 to 222 BCE, Rome fought the Gauls in northern Italy and looked to expand into the territory of Illyria across the Adriatic Sea. However, things would take a turn, which would set Carthage and Rome once again against each other in a fight for their very existence.

Chapter Seven: Hannibal Ad Portas ("Hannibal Is at the Gates!")

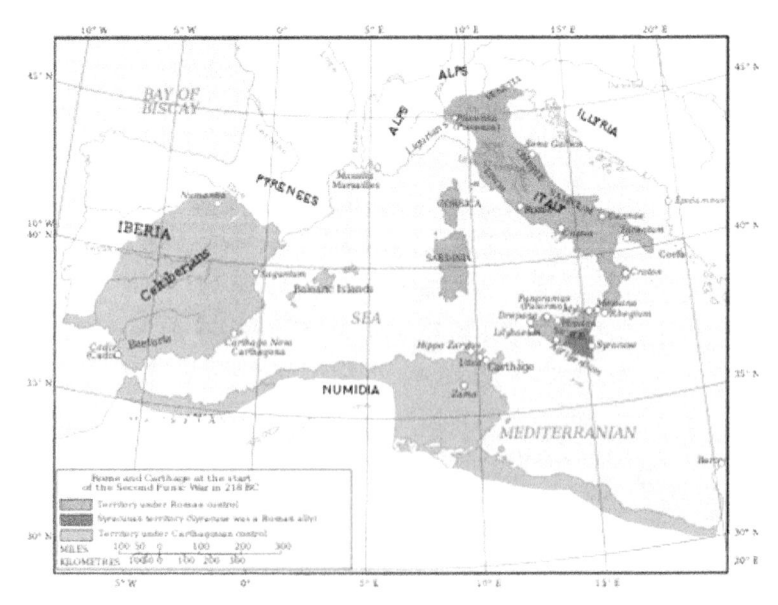

Carthage and Rome at the beginning of the Second Punic War.
*Grandiosederivative work : Augusta 89, CC BY-SA 3.0
<https://creativecommons.org/licenses/by-sa/3.0>, via Wikimedia Commons;
https://commons.wikimedia.org/wiki/File:Map_of_Rome_and_Carthage_at_the_start_of_the_Second_Punic_War_2.svg*

The "Mercenary War" that erupted just after the end of the First Punic War was significant in many ways. Hamilcar Barca retired from his role as commander of the Carthaginian military after securing the peace treaty with Rome, perhaps because he had been unhappy with the Carthaginian surrender. Another Carthaginian commander, Gisco, had the task of sending the many mercenaries employed by Carthage back to Cape Bon, where they expected to receive their payment. Carthage, most likely owing to a lack of currency, delayed handing out payments but instead sent the mercenaries to a town called Sicca.

As the mercenary numbers grew and as time drew on, the soldiers had plenty of free time to tally up just how much they thought the Carthaginians owed them, usually arriving at exceedingly large amounts. Feeling that the Carthaginians were ignoring their demands and because the mercenaries spoke a myriad of languages, which made it difficult for the Carthaginians to communicate with them, the mercenaries began to speak of rebellion. They were led by two mercenaries named Spendius and Mathos; they demanded that Gisco come to them and deal with them directly. The Carthaginians agreed to this, but the mercenaries captured Gisco and his guards and held them as prisoners.

Spendius and Mathos were able to gain the support of the Libyan subjects of Carthage, who had been heavily taxed by the Carthaginians during the First Punic War. Thus, the Mercenary War began, and Carthage, wanting nothing more than peace after its long years at war with Rome, found itself almost immediately in another struggle.

The mercenary and Libyan armies then set about besieging Utica and Hippo, close neighbors of Carthage. The Carthaginians suffered many losses early on and eventually recalled Hamilcar Barca to lead their forces. He moved quickly and ended the siege on Utica. He then met the army of Spendius in a field near Carthage and defeated him soundly. Mathos continued to besiege Hippo while Spendius escaped to Tunis. A group of Numidians from North Africa, led by a man named Naravas, came to offer their services to Hannibal Barca, who, despite his successes, was still outnumbered by the combined forces of Mathos and

Spendius. Barca welcomed Naravas and promised him his daughter's hand in marriage if the Numidians assisted him.

Bust of Hannibal Barca.
https://commons.wikimedia.org/wiki/File:Mommsen_p265.jpg

Hamilcar treated any prisoners he captured well, offering them the chance to return home or join his army. Spendius and Mathos became concerned this would lead to the disintegration of their forces, so they began to convince their confederates that Hamilcar's actions were a ruse. One of their commanders, a Gaul named Autaritus, encouraged the idea and convinced Spendius to have seven hundred prisoners, including the Carthaginian commander Gesco, tortured and killed by cutting off their hands and then extremities before finally dispatching them. When knowledge of this reached the Carthaginians, they became incensed and knew they could no longer give leniency to the rebels. In 239 BCE, the loyal cities of Utica and Hippacritae killed those in the Carthaginian garrisons and joined the rebels. The rebels then began to besiege Carthage itself.

The rebels ran out of supplies and were forced to end the siege of Carthage and fall back to Tunis. However, Spendius took an army of forty thousand men and harassed Hamilcar's army but eventually became pinned against a mountain range called the Saw. They ran out of supplies and were forced to eat their horses, then their prisoners, and then their slaves. Spendius and his lieutenants came to a parlay with Hamilcar but were arrested. The rest of the army attacked and were killed to the last man. Hamilcar had Spendius and his surviving officers crucified in front of Tunis, where Mathos remained.

Upon seeing the situation, Mathos left Tunis and met Hamilcar and another commander, Hanno, in battle at Leptis Parva. No details of the battle survive, but the rebels were crushed. Mathos was taken prisoner and dragged through the streets of Carthage, where he was tortured and then killed by the inhabitants. All of the cities that had sided with the rebels were won back by the Carthaginians, including Utica and Hippo.

The Mercenary War had unintended consequences that would prove pivotal to how Carthage planned to rebuild itself. In 240 or 239 BCE, the Carthaginian garrisons on the island of Sardinia had joined the mutiny, effectively ending Carthaginian control of this important island. When the Carthaginians sent a force to retake the island, that force joined the mutiny, and all the loyal Carthaginians on the island were killed. The rebels on Sardinia appealed to Rome for help, but Rome refused. In 237 BCE, the indigenous people of Sardinia rose up and took the island back, forcing the rebels to flee. These people then appealed to Rome. Rome accepted and took control of Sardinia. Carthage protested, stating that it was putting together a force to retake the island. Rome considered this an act of war and demanded that Carthage hand over control of Sardinia and Corsica and pay another 1,200 talents to Rome. After thirty years of war, the Carthaginians did not have the spirit to continue fighting, so they agreed to Rome's demands.

Hamilcar Barca, thus having regained North Africa for the Carthaginians, was sent to the Iberian Peninsula to expand and secure territories there. He brought his nine-year-old son, Hannibal, with him. Barca met his end in battle, and the command of the army in Spain went to his son-in-law, Hasdrubal. Hasdrubal ruled in Spain for eight years. He was able to expand Carthaginian territory mostly by means of diplomacy. He was assassinated by a Celt for what was said to have been something of a private nature. The command then fell to young Hannibal, the son of the great Hamilcar Barca.

According to ancient sources on the subject, upon taking the mantle of command, Hannibal had every intention of rekindling the war with Rome. The Carthaginians, for their part, felt abused by Rome in the ensuing peace, while the Romans remained suspicious that the Carthaginians would try to reclaim their empire.

Hasdrubal's and Hannibal's ascensions were a clear display of how things had changed politically in the Carthaginian world. When Hamilcar Barca died, his successor would have previously been picked by the Council of Elders in Carthage, but the Barcid clan had established so much dominance in southern Spain that the Carthaginian army took it upon itself to declare Hasdrubal the new leader of the army. The Public Assembly in Carthage, which supported the Barcids completely, quickly approved the appointment. The same thing happened when Hasdrubal was killed; the army declared Hannibal the new commander, and the Public Assembly approved the decision, bypassing the Council of Elders completely.

Hannibal was, in everything but name, the king of a region that encompassed much of southern Spain. He ruled from a palace in a city his brother-in-law had founded called New Carthage, modern-day Cartagena. While Barcid Spain enjoyed a silver boon and quickly paid off Carthage's debt to Rome with plenty to spare, the archaeological evidence shows Carthage remained in an economic slump during this time.

In 221 BCE, twenty-six-year-old Hannibal Barca took power. There were plenty in the Carthaginian elite who resented the apparent unregulated power of the Barcids. The coins minted in

Barcid Spain during this time show a clean-shaven Hercules-Melqart with a club and laurel leaves on one side and an African elephant on the other—a reference to Hannibal's father and the Barcid clan in general. Hannibal spent the first two years as general dealing with issues in Spain and expanding Carthaginian control to the northwest, fighting the Celtiberians.

Early on, it became clear that Hannibal was as good a general, if not greater, than his famous father. In the spring of 220 BCE, Hannibal was faced with a force of Celtiberians greater than his own. He feigned a retreat across a river and set up camp. When the enemy took the bait, they crossed the river only to be ambushed by Hannibal's cavalry. The ones that made it through were then crushed by forty war elephants. Hannibal easily crossed the river and finished off the rest of the enemy's forces.

Hannibal then crossed the Hiberus River (modern-day Ebro River), took much of the territory there, and headed toward the city of Saguntum, which was a Roman ally. A debate arose within the city between pro-Roman and pro-Barcid factions. Roman envoys within the city, of course, sided with the pro-Roman faction and had many from the other side executed. The message was clear: an attack on Saguntum was a provocation of war.

Hannibal tightened his hold on the land surrounding the city, and the people of Saguntum sent appeals to Rome, which responded by sending emissaries to meet with Hannibal directly. The Romans, having kept abreast of Carthaginian activity in Iberia, knew they should talk with Hannibal and not waste time meeting with anyone in Carthage itself. The Romans met with Hannibal in his palace at New Carthage and told him plainly that he should not interfere in Saguntum. Hannibal replied that Rome had been the first to interfere in Saguntum, referencing the execution of pro-Carthaginians. He told the Romans that it was a Carthaginian tradition not to overlook injustice. The Romans stormed off and traveled to Carthage to express their protests there.

Hannibal was in a fine position to deal so high-handedly with the Romans. He personally controlled a vast territory in Spain that provided him with plenty of food and more than enough silver to pay his troops. He had a seasoned army of sixty thousand infantry, eight thousand cavalry, and two hundred war elephants. He was allied with many of the leaders around him, and he had married an Iberian to secure his political position. With this in mind, he disregarded the Roman threats and attacked Saguntum. It took eighteen months to conquer the city, during which Rome sent more envoys to Hannibal, but he sent them away without seeing them. The Romans who went to Carthage demanded to know if Hannibal's actions were sanctioned by the government. The Carthaginians deflected. The Romans asked if Carthage wanted peace or war; once again, the Carthaginians turned the question back on the envoys. The Romans decided on war, thus beginning the Second Punic War in 218 BCE.

It is believed that Hasdrubal had planned on crossing from Iberia into Gaul and then crossing the Alps, where he hoped to meet up with the Cisalpine Gauls to attack Rome. However, Rome had conquered the Gauls in northern Italy, and Hasdrubal had been assassinated, so Rome might have believed the threat had been avoided. However, Hannibal clearly wanted to continue where his brother-in-law had left off. After taking Saguntum, he sent plunder to Carthage, which gained him plenty of supporters there, though Hanno II, an old rival of Hannibal's father, voiced his opposition to the Barcids. He told the Council of Elders that Hannibal wished nothing more than to be a king and that as long as a Barcid controlled the army, there would never be peace with Rome. His words had no impact, if for no other reason than Hannibal controlled Spain, which had become Carthage's most profitable territory. The tribes in Iberia had pledged allegiance to the Barcids, not Carthage. Hannibal could not be detained or replaced. Wherever he went, Carthage went.

Rome was not yet ready to mobilize an army, and it had no idea what Hannibal had planned. Hannibal took his time after the fall of Saguntum to build up his army and stores for the grueling ordeal ahead. Hannibal left his brother, Hasdrubal, in Spain to defend it in case of a Roman attack and to keep the locals under a watchful eye.

Hannibal's plan sounded fairly straightforward. He would go by land north to Gaul and then east, thereby entering Italy from the north. This overland route would offer Hannibal the element of surprise because the Romans would not imagine Hannibal's army crossing both the Pyrenees and the Alps, the two highest mountain ranges in western Europe, to make war with them. It was a daring and incredibly risky plan, but Hannibal was a bold commander, and he knew this sort of gambit could provide a great payout.

Also, he did not have many options. After the end of the First Punic War, Rome's rule of the sea was unquestioned in the western Mediterranean. The Punic fleet at the outbreak of Hannibal's war was only thirty-seven ships. Furthermore, Hannibal was a land commander; he had no great admirals to rely on.

In 218 BCE, the Roman consuls were Publius Cornelius Scipio and Tiberius Sempronius Longus. Their plan was for Scipio to take 22,000 infantry and 2,200 cavalry and go to Spain to battle Hannibal, whom they assumed would still be there, while Longus took 27,000 men and a fleet of 180 ships to invade Africa.

Hannibal began his campaign by swiftly taking several cities and conquering tribes in modern-day Catalonia. This was particularly important because some of these tribes were known to be on friendly terms with the Romans. At that time, Hannibal then had about fifty thousand infantry, nine thousand cavalry, and several hundred war elephants. He split his force into three columns, which each crossed the Ebro River. The crossing of the river and subduing the tribes in the area took a total of two months, during which Hannibal lost an estimated thirteen thousand men. The march through the Pyrenees and down to the Rhone River was largely uneventful. Publius Scipio had been given orders by the Senate to divert his course and meet Hannibal in northwest Spain, but he was not quick enough and missed the enemy. He learned in Massalia (modern-day Marseille) that Hannibal was not in Catalonia as he expected but was four days away from the Rhone.

The Romans attempted to meet Hannibal as he crossed the Rhone River. However, Hannibal was already making the crossing from the west bank. On the east bank was a Gallic tribe called the Cavares, who were prepared to attack the Carthaginian army when it crossed. However, Hannibal took Alexander the Great as his model, remembering when the Macedonian king crossed the Hydaspes River in India. Hannibal had one of his commanders take a northern route around the Cavares and attack their flank just as Hannibal's main army was making the crossing. In this way, Hannibal was able to crush the Cavares and cross the river without issue.

Hannibal had to get from the Rhone to the Alps as quickly as possible so that he would be able to cross the mountains before winter set in. If he could not do it in time, then the element of surprise would be lost, and the Romans would be able to raise an army to stop him from entering Italy. He had his cavalry skirt his right flank, which was the side near the sea, as he believed the Romans might land boats and attack from that direction. The cavalry could then hold the enemy off while Hannibal's infantry formed their lines. Hannibal stayed in the rear of his force with the war elephants, which now numbered thirty-seven, as he also believed the Romans might be behind him and come from that direction. The cavalry traveled about nineteen miles a day, while the infantry traveled twelve miles a day. For an ancient army traversing rough and unknown terrain, this was an exceptional speed.

Hannibal's army eventually reached the Alps. The route he took is still hotly debated, as it was in ancient times. There are at least five popular theories, with many other acceptable theories as well. It is believed that he might have taken the Little St. Bernard Pass, which goes from Savoie, France, to the Aosta Valley in Italy. The modern road that now goes across this pass is closed from November to the end of April. He also might have taken the Col de Clapier from Savoie, France, to the Piedmont region of Italy. There is the Col de la Traversette, where sediments appear to have been churned up around approximately the early 3rd century BCE; however, no Carthaginian artifacts have been found, nor the tell-tale bones of elephants. Another theory suggests Col de Montgenèvre, which was known to the Romans and would eventually be used by Julius Caesar when he began his campaign into Gaul. Also, there was a pass that went from Val-Cenis in France to Susa in Italy. Currently, there is no definitive answer.

The consul Publius arrived at the Rhone and found that the Carthaginian army had already crossed. By then, he could have figured out what Hannibal's plan was. He also would have been aware that the Carthaginian general was carrying out his strategy with great speed. Publius sent his brother to continue attacking the Carthaginians in Spain, while he planned to return to Italy and meet Hannibal when he descended the Alps.

Hannibal's journey through the Alps has become something more legendary than real, but it was certainly done, and it must have been a grueling ordeal for everyone involved, including the animals. Snow had begun to fall in many places. Men and beasts slipped from high paths and were dashed on the rocks below. Hannibal's ability to keep his men marching and to stop any mutinous actions is a testament to his ability as a leader. Many of the men in the army had never seen snow and had never crossed such mountains; it must have seemed impossible to them, but Hannibal kept them moving forward.

The men did not only have to contend with just the climate and terrain. They were also dogged by local tribes who hoped to gain booty and remove the outsiders from their homeland. Yet, as the Carthaginians rose higher in the mountains, these attacks stopped because they had reached a land where no man lived. They finally reached the crest of a huge mountain, where Hannibal was soon able to show his men the Po Valley stretching out before them. There, he told them, was where they would defeat their eternal enemy, the Romans. The spirits of his men lifted, and they began the dangerous task of descending the Alps.

When Hannibal's army reached the Po Valley and completed the crossing of the Alps, they numbered twenty thousand infantry, six thousand cavalry, and an unknown number of war elephants, which were now sick and famished after the crossing. They descended sometime in the fall of 218 BCE. After a short period of rest, the Carthaginians attacked the hostile Taurini, a Celtic-Ligurian tribe. They defeated them and raided their food stores. In late November, Publius Scipio and Hannibal met in battle. This would be the first time Hannibal faced Roman forces on Italian soil. It was at first a cavalry battle, with Hannibal having strength in numbers, but Scipio believed his soldiers were the better fighters.

When they met, a melee broke out. Hannibal's Numidian cavalry outflanked Scipio's men, causing the Romans to crumble and flee. Hannibal returned to his army and prepared for the main battle, thinking the cavalry battle was only a skirmish, but Scipio, perhaps feeling his men had lost morale, retreated down the Po River. This was not just a defeat for the Romans; the battle also caused all the local Gallic tribes to side with the Carthaginians. Hannibal's army increased dramatically in size after the Battle of Ticinus. The significance of this victory cannot be overstated.

Scipio fell back to the Trebia River, and Hannibal followed. Meanwhile, the Roman Senate had made the decision to abandon the plan for Consul Tiberius Sempronius Longus to attempt an invasion of Africa, instead ordering Longus to turn back from Sicily and come to Scipio's aid. Longus acted quickly and arrived at Scipio's camp before Hannibal could attack. The Romans are believed to have had about thirty-eight thousand infantry and four thousand cavalry. The Carthaginians had about twenty-nine thousand infantry and eleven thousand cavalry.

Since both consuls were with the Roman army, they alternated leadership every other day and camped in separate locations. Hannibal used this to his advantage. He waited until the inexperienced and rash Longus was in command to begin his attack. Scipio, who had been injured in the earlier engagement, had wanted to wait until after winter to battle Hannibal, but Longus wanted the glory of defeating the dreaded Carthaginian general.

On the morning of the Battle of Trebia, Hannibal sent out his Numidian cavalry to provoke the Romans. Longus fell for the trap in his eagerness to fight the Carthaginians. He sent his whole army after the Numidians, who wheeled around and took their positions at the wings of Hannibal's army. The Romans crossed the chest-high Trebia River, which was icy cold. The Carthaginians held back and waited for the Romans to come. The outcome was almost predictable. The infantry in the center met, and the fighting was fierce, with the Romans getting the better of it. However, the Carthaginian cavalry wings defeated the Roman cavalry quickly.

Meanwhile, a contingent of two thousand troops commanded by another of Hannibal's brothers, Mago, revealed themselves from their hiding spot to the rear of the Romans and attacked the unguarded rear infantry. The Romans broke and began to flee. The Roman death toll was estimated to be about fifteen thousand, which was a huge loss. Still, the fighting had been rough, and the Carthaginians lost about five thousand men, men that would be harder to replace than the Romans considering their location. Still, no matter how Sempronius Longus presented the battle to the Senate, it was clearly a devastating defeat. Both armies settled down to their winter quarters to wait for the spring.

Meanwhile, Gnaeus Cornelius Scipio, brother of Publius Scipio, landed with his fleet on the coast of Spain and began to attack cities allied with the Carthaginians. He was able to capture a Carthaginian general and an Iberian despot. Hannibal's brother, Hasdrubal, heard of these attacks and ventured north, destroying Roman ships and securing cities that had been taken by the Romans, although he did not face Gnaeus in open battle yet. Instead, he retreated south of the Ebro River and camped for the winter. Gnaeus Scipio stayed north of the Ebro and also settled down for the winter.

During the winter, Hannibal took various precautions to ensure his army would be ready come the spring. He was particularly concerned about the attitude of the northern Italian Gauls who surrounded him, some of whom had recently joined his army. He treated his Roman prisoners poorly, but he treated the Gallic prisoners well and eventually freed them to return to their homes. By doing this, he hoped to encourage support from the local tribes. However, Hannibal was aware that there might be spies and assassins in his midst, so he had several different wigs made of many different colors, which he would change regularly, along with different clothes so that people could not even recognize him easily. While Hannibal managed to survive the winter, along with most of his army, his war elephants did not do so well. When the weather changed, and it was time once again to be on the march, only one elephant remained.

In the spring of 217 BCE, Hannibal decided to head south. The new Roman consuls, Gnaeus Servilius and Gaius Flaminius, had separate armies and were prepared to stop Hannibal through the eastern or western route to Rome. Hannibal, however, decided to take a more difficult but more direct route through the mouth of the Arno River, which was a large marshland. The way was hard, especially on his Gallic allies, and because much of the land they crossed was covered in water, they were unable to sleep for days on end. Hannibal even lost his right eye from conjunctivitis during the journey.

The army arrived in Etruria. Hannibal wanted to lure Flaminius's army out of their encampment by destroying much of the land that they were supposed to protect. Hannibal attacked locations behind Flaminius's defensive position in an effort to draw him out of his protected location. Flaminius eventually realized he could not just sit passively by and went in pursuit of Hannibal. The Carthaginian army ambushed the Romans in a narrow pass on the shores of Lake Trasimene.

The Carthaginian army made camp but conducted tricky night marches to array themselves along the ridge above a narrow pass. Flaminius did not send scouts out before marching into the pass, which was not particularly unordinary. Hannibal waited until the Romans were fully within the trap before letting his soldiers loose. The combined Gallic, Iberian, and African forces slammed into the side and rear of the unexpecting Romans and decimated them. Of the twenty-five thousand Romans involved, only a few thousand escaped with their lives. Flaminius was supposedly killed by a Gaul. Gnaeus's cavalry units, which were unaware of what had happened to Flaminius's army, were scouting ahead when they were also defeated by Hannibal's forces a few days after the Battle of Lake Trasimene. Gnaeus pulled back his forces and retreated to Ariminum, modern-day Rimini, on the Adriatic coast.

When the news of the battle's outcome reached Rome, the city was overcome with panic. Fearing that Hannibal would arrive at the gates of Rome any day, the Romans took drastic measures. They dismissed the idea of electing new consuls but instead appointed a dictator: Quintus Fabius Maximus. He came from the esteemed Fabia clan, which claimed descent from Hercules and was among the first followers of Romulus and Remus, the legendary founders of Rome. Although Quintus Fabius was a dictator, he was not allowed to select his second-in-command. The Romans appointed a political rival, Marcus Minucius Rufus, to that position.

Hannibal, however, decided not to besiege Rome. After the march through the marshland and the subsequent battles, he knew his men and horses needed rest. He marched to the Adriatic and settled there for some time to feed his soldiers and animals from the abundant produce of the area. He also equipped some of his army with the weapons and armor they had taken from the Romans. A message was sent to Carthage, giving the details of his campaign and his victories against the Romans. The people of Carthage were elated and sent troops to both Spain and Italy. Hannibal then marched his army across Italy, devastating the countryside.

In the meantime, Fabius had been able to muster four legions for the emergency and marched out of Rome to Rimini, where he relieved Gnaeus of command and sent him back to Rome to prepare for any possible Carthaginian attacks by sea. Fabius then approached Hannibal's army and set up camp. Upon seeing the Romans, Hannibal brought his army out and arrayed his men for battle, but the Romans did not come out to meet him. Fabius had learned from his predecessor's mistakes. He adopted a strategy in which he would not meet Hannibal in all-out combat but would attack his supply lines and harass the enemy in a war of attrition. This would eventually be called the "Fabian strategy." The Carthaginians were an army prepared for battle, and their success lay in victory on the battlefield. Fabius realized that the Romans were in an entirely different position. They had almost limitless supplies and men but would almost certainly be defeated in a traditional engagement. However, Fabius's second-in-command, Marcus, openly criticized the dictator for what he considered to be weakness and cowardice.

Hannibal did everything he could to try and draw Fabius into a battle. He even ravaged all the land around Fabius's country estate but left the dictator's land untouched, adding to a rumor that Fabius was somehow working with Hannibal. However, a year passed without a decisive battle.

In the following year, 216 BCE, Fabius's dictatorship ended, and the Romans mustered eighty-seven thousand troops. The Romans elected two consuls: Gaius Terentius Varro and Lucius Aemilius Paullus, who had opposing views on how the war with

Hannibal should be conducted. Paullus favored the Fabian strategy, but Varro wanted to defeat the Carthaginians once and for all. Eventually, in late July, the Roman army tracked Hannibal down to a small town named Cannae. On August 1st, Hannibal offered to engage the Romans in an open battle, but Paullus was in command that day and refused. On the next day, he offered the same again; Varro was more than willing to meet the Carthaginian army.

The Romans established themselves in a linear formation, while Hannibal put his troops in a crescent shape, with his least reliable soldiers in the center. The Romans pushed through the center but then found themselves enveloped by the Carthaginian forces, who then closed in and defeated the numerically superior Romans. The loss at the Battle of Cannae did not decide the war but caused some Italian allies to abandon Rome and go over to the Carthaginian side. With this victory, the road to Rome now lay open, but it appears Hannibal's primary goal was not to lay siege to Rome, which would be long and costly. He certainly wanted to continue to win over Rome's allies in Italy, but it seems that he sought to establish terms of peace after Cannae since he sent several messengers to Rome to ransom prisoners. However, Rome rejected the offer and forbade the paying of ransoms for prisoners and publicly announced its intention to fight until the bitter end.

For the next few years, things followed a similar pattern. Rome continued to levy more troops, eventually allowing criminals and the poor to be soldiers. In 214 BCE, the Romans had eighteen legions; the next year, they had twenty-two. In total, Rome had about 100,000 soldiers, not counting allied troops, but they were broken up into forces of about 20,000. Thus, they could not face Hannibal directly but were able to hamper his movements. Most of southern Italy, which had formerly been Greek cities, went over to the Carthaginian side. Macedonia sent emissaries and established an alliance with Hannibal. There was even a pro-Carthaginian rebellion in Sardinia, but the Romans were able to stamp it out quickly.

Fabius became consul and continued his strategy. Eleven years after Cannae, war raged around southern Italy. In 207 BCE,

Hasdrubal Barca followed his brother and crossed the Alps into Cisalpine Gaul. In 205 BCE, another of Hannibal's brothers, Mago Barca, landed his troops in northwest Italy after he had been defeated by Roman forces in Iberia.

However, in 204 BCE, Publius Cornelius Scipio, the Roman general that had defeated Mago, carried out his planned invasion of Africa. Scipio was the son of a former consul also named Publius Cornelius Scipio, who had died fighting Hasdrubal Barca in Spain. He was the only person to ask to command the army in Spain, as it was considered unwinnable. After defeating Mago, Scipio rejected the idea of returning to Italy, instead feeling the best option was to take the war to Carthage. When he arrived in Africa, the Numidian commander, Masinissa, allied with the Romans. Scipio quickly defeated two Carthaginian armies. Due to this sudden change in events and the fact that the city was in danger of being taken, Carthage recalled Hannibal and Mago back to Africa. Hannibal and Scipio met at the Battle of Zama in 202 BCE.

Hannibal had thirty-six thousand infantry, four thousand cavalry, and eighty war elephants. Scipio commanded twenty-nine thousand infantry and over six thousand cavalry. They both deployed their infantry in the center in three lines and their cavalry in the wings. Scipio and Hannibal had both studied each other and knew their strengths and weaknesses. Hannibal held back his center to avoid being encircled by Scipio's wings. Scipio knew that the war elephants could charge but only in straight lines. So, he had his men leave gaps in their lines where they could let the elephants pass through without doing any real damage.

The fighting was fierce; it seemed Hannibal had certainly met his match in Scipio. The Carthaginian cavalry was routed, and the Roman cavalry was able to encircle Hannibal's army. Hannibal was finally defeated. It was the end of the Second Punic War.

Chapter Eight: Carthago Delenda Est ("Carthage Must Be Destroyed")

Hannibal was able to escape the Romans. He went to Carthage and advised the Council of Elders to begin peace negotiations immediately. The peace terms the Romans proposed included the loss of all territory outside their home in North Africa. Additionally, Carthage was forbidden from fighting any wars outside Africa and even then had to seek permission from Rome. The indemnity was a hefty ten thousand talents of silver to be paid over fifty years. That was ten times the amount in the treaty of 241 BCE. Carthage also had to give up its war elephants and could have no more than ten warships. The Council of Elders accepted the terms. Scipio would forever bear the name "Africanus" for his conquests on the continent. The Roman Senate approved the terms, and the treaty was ratified in North Africa. Carthage's fleet was burned before the city, and Scipio returned to Rome, where he enjoyed a triumph.

Hannibal remained in charge of part of his army, which he set to work planting olive orchards. He then entered politics. Hannibal soon gained popularity among the common citizens by correcting corruption within the government. He proposed a new law in which members of the Council of the Hundred and Four would be decided by elections. He then conducted an audit of state revenues and found evidence of embezzlement from officials. As a result, Hannibal soon made enemies with the political elite. He was a populist leader and began a construction program to improve the city.

The Council of Elders began to be concerned that Hannibal was attempting an autocratic takeover of Carthage. The council sent reports to Rome, saying that Hannibal was scheming with the enemy, Antiochus of the Seleucid Empire. Roman envoys arrived to investigate, and Hannibal fled to the court of Antiochus, as it was the only place he could find safety.

Once there, Hannibal proposed an attack on the Italian Peninsula. The Carthaginians once again sent reports to Rome of Hannibal's activities, and he found himself on the outskirts of Antiochus's court. The Seleucids attempted to expand their empire but were defeated by the Romans in 190 BCE, so Hannibal once again fled, drifting to and from various Hellenistic courts. He finally arrived in Bithynia, but his presence was discovered by the Roman general Titus Quinctius Flamininus. Before he could be handed over to the Romans by Bithynian soldiers, he took the poison he always carried with him. Hannibal died in 181 BCE.

In 180 BCE, Carthage made a remarkable recovery, as it had been freed from the troubles of empire-building and war. The Carthaginians were able to settle their debt to Rome after only ten years, but the Romans denied their request. Carthage was able to supply millions of bushels of grain to Rome and certainly had plenty left over. Carthage's agricultural economy grew rapidly, while Rome had to rely on help from allies due to constant warfare. The Carthaginians also improved their shipyards. The circular port was able to hold at least 170 vessels, though this would have been far beyond what had been stipulated in the peace treaty made with Rome.

It seems these harbors, which were possibly built at this time, were created to be invisible from the seaside of the city. The port was built far inland and would have been impossible to see from ships sailing past the city. Still, the Romans had emissaries who entered the city regularly and would have known about the construction of these harbors. It seems more likely that the inner harbor was not used exclusively for warships but also for Carthage's commercial fleet.

Carthage had a bigger problem with King Masinissa, the Numidian who had been of such great service to Scipio. Masinissa, as a Numidian, was certainly jealous of Carthage's power and took advantage of the results of the Second Punic War to grow his power. He used his position to keep the Romans wary and suspicious of the Carthaginians. Masinissa often seized some of the agricultural output of North Africa as his own. Tensions between Carthage and Numidia resulted in envoys being sent to Rome, but Rome tended to almost always favor their allies, the Numidians. In fact, one of Masinissa's sons, Gulussa, traveled to Rome to tell the Senate to beware of Carthage, which he said was preparing a large fleet to defeat the Romans. This accusation never came to anything, but it helped fuel the fire of anti-Carthaginian attitudes in Rome.

In 162 BCE, Masinissa overran farmland in Syrtis Minor, a territory that Carthage had owned for centuries. Rome ruled in favor of the Numidian king and forced Carthage to hand over the trading towns along the coast and pay the Numidians five hundred talents as well. Masinissa did this again with some land in the Thusca region. Carthage once again complained to Rome.

Rome sent an envoy led by Marcus Porcius Cato, who was eighty-one years old at the time. Cato had served in the Second Punic War, and his hatred for Carthage was as strong as his political will. He arrived in Carthage in 152 BCE. Cato ruled in favor of Numidia, but he was also appalled by what he found in Carthage. The city was teeming with vigorous men and overflowing with wealth. There were weapons of every description. He saw crops growing in abundance in the countryside. The envoys found stored timber, which they believed might be for the warships Carthage was supposed to be building.

When Cato returned to Rome, he set about convincing his fellow senators of what actions needed to be taken. He ended every speech with "Carthago delenda est" or "Carthage must be destroyed." He felt that Carthage was not only on the verge of building back its armies and wealth but that it had also learned from its previous mistakes and would annihilate Rome. Cato was opposed by a faction led by Scipio Nasica, nephew of Scipio Africanus, who believed that the complete destruction of Carthage would destroy Rome's equilibrium. Without a clear adversary, Rome would become drunk with greed and power. It is from later writers that we hear of Scipio Nasica's arguments, and those later writers, of course, knew that the Roman Republic would eventually fall into civil war, with the republic being replaced by an empire. Scipio might have simply felt that there was no clear justification for war against Carthage. But this did not seem to concern Cato.

By the end of the 150s BCE, it had become clear to Carthage that its treaty with Rome offered no protection but only obligations. The Carthaginians could not rely on Rome to help them in their dealings with the Numidians. A group led by Hamilcar the Samnite and Carthalo gained popular support in Carthage for their belief that the city needed to defend itself. Masinissa sent two of his sons to demand that pro-Numidian leaders be established in the city. His sons were not allowed in Carthage, so they were ambushed by Hamilcar. War was declared between Carthage and Numidia.

After a brief battle, the Carthaginians were surrounded, starved out, and then massacred. Masinissa took another large piece of Carthaginian territory as a result. The greater issue was that the Carthaginians had violated the peace terms established in 201 BCE; they had declared war without Rome's approval. Rome had since resolved its wars in Macedon and Greece, so it now had a large army it could use to attack Carthage and answer Cato's demands. In 150 BCE, Rome mobilized an army for North Africa. Carthage sent envoys to Rome, but by the time they got to Italy, the army had already set out for Sicily. The Carthaginian envoys were greeted with a cool welcome. When they explained that they were going to execute those who had led the war against Numidia, the Romans asked why they were not already dead. When the Carthaginians asked what they could do to atone for their crimes, the Senate told them simply that they must satisfy the Roman people. Cato rallied the Senate, demanding to know why they should forgive Carthage after all the times its people had acted cruelly and broken trust with Rome.

Rome, putting up a farce of possible reconciliation, asked Carthage for three hundred noble children as a sign of good faith. At the same time, an army of eighty thousand infantry and four thousand cavalry, led by consuls Lucius Marcius Censorinus and Manius Manilius, was headed to North Africa. The army disembarked at Utica and told the Carthaginians how war could be avoided. The Carthaginians sent envoys and were told by the consuls that they must surrender all their weapons. Carthage handed over weapons for twenty thousand men and two thousand large catapults. The Romans then told them they could live freely under their own laws but that they must move their city and allow the current one to be destroyed. The envoys tried to argue against this destruction, but their pleas fell on deaf ears. They had to return to Carthage to deliver the unfortunate news that the city they loved would be razed to the ground.

However, the Carthaginians would not accept Rome's terms, and they began to prepare for war. Every building was turned into a workshop to make weapons. Women cut their hair for rope to make catapults. All the slaves were freed, and Hasdrubal, who had escaped execution, was placed in charge of the entire operation. Rome prepared to besiege the city. The siege began in 149 but dragged into 148 BCE. Hasdrubal had been able to get his army out of the city and was disrupting Roman supply lines in the Carthaginian hinterland. Thus, the Romans were still unsuccessful in 147 BCE.

But this was the year that Scipio Aemilianus, the adopted grandson of Scipio Africanus, rose to the consulship and was put in charge of the African campaign. Scipio acted quickly and corrected what he felt was lax discipline within the Roman ranks. He centered his army around Carthage and led a daring night attack with four thousand men. His forces were able to get past the defenses and enter the city. However, he soon realized his position was undefendable, so he returned to the rest of his army.

Things within the city had deteriorated, though. Realizing that there was no chance for surrender, anyone who spoke against those in charge was put to death. Roman prisoners were killed on the city walls in full view of the Roman army. Scipio attempted to cut off Carthage's harbor by building a large mole, or causeway, across it, but the Carthaginians simply dug another trench from the harbor to the sea. A newly built navy sailed out of this opening and attacked the Roman ships in the Battle of the Port of Carthage, but it was forced to withdraw. Many ships sank or were captured. Scipio also attacked the Carthaginian army in the field, overran its camp, and killed many of the soldiers.

Scipio's command was extended for another year. In the spring of 146 BCE, he launched a full-scale assault that successfully breached the city walls. Over the next six days, the Romans and Carthaginians fought in the streets, setting fire to many of the buildings. There was a terrible slaughter until Scipio began to allow the Carthaginians to surrender themselves instead of simply killing them. This was true except for nine hundred Roman deserters who were trapped in the temple of Eshmun. The deserters, knowing all hope was lost, set fire to the temple and died inside.

The Carthaginian leader, Hasdrubal, eventually surrendered to Scipio. Upon seeing this, his wife took his children into a burning building as she cursed her husband. This was not just the end of the Third Punic War but also the end of ancient Carthage, one of the greatest cities in the western Mediterranean and once the center of a great empire. Carthage would lay in ruins for a hundred years, only to be rebuilt as a Roman city. The city survived into the Middle Ages, but it was never truly Carthage again.

Chapter Nine: Government and Military

Like any other nation or empire, the Carthaginian government and military changed over time. In the beginning, it was believed Carthage was an oligarchic government. The city was ruled by an aristocratic elite called the *b'lm*, or the princes. This group controlled every important judicial, governmental, religious, and military decision in the state. The ancient Greeks apparently believed the Carthaginians were ruled by kings, but this seems to have been a misunderstanding, probably due to the fact that the princes were led by a single dynastic family, such as the Magonids or Barcids. The Carthaginians seemed to have a tendency to give political power to a son after the father had died, but it was different from a monarchy, in which power automatically went from father to son, etc. There was not a clear line of succession in Carthage. We can see this when Hamilcar Barca died; instead of power going directly to Hannibal, it instead went to his older and presumably more competent brother-in-law, Hasdrubal. It was not until Hasdrubal was assassinated that Hannibal was able to gain power.

Even when a son rose to be the greatest among the princes, he was not an autocratic ruler. There were various councils that were able to, more or less, check his power. There was, of course, the Popular Assembly, which appears to have been a part of

Carthage's political landscape sometime after the loss of Syracuse to Gelon, but it initially did not have much power. This body was composed of citizens of Carthage, and there were various qualifications that changed over the years, such as age, property ownership, and wealth. However, the particulars of who could and could not participate in the Popular Assembly are not completely known due to the loss of all of Carthage's records when the city was burned by the Romans. However, the Popular Assembly saw a great increase in power thanks to the rise of the Barcids after the Sicilian Wars. Hamilcar was able to secure the general command of an army in Libya simply by popular vote, something that would have been unheard of a generation before. The ordinary citizen, or *s'rnm*, now had a taste of influence that they would not give up.

There was also the Council of Elders, which seems to have been a very old institution within the city. This was, as the name suggests, a council of venerated older members of the elite class whose power waxed and waned as the years went by. They could decide who controlled the army and conducted foreign affairs and had control of the treasury.

After the loss of Syracuse to Gelon, another council was formed: the Council of the Hundred and Four. This council appointed special commissioners, called *pentarchies*, who dealt with a wide range of affairs of state. The Hundred and Four was a council of judges that, according to Aristotle, were the highest constitutional authority. They had the ability to judge generals, along with many other powers. This was particularly important because generals had a great deal of autonomy in the Carthaginian government, and the Hundred and Four provided a check to their power. The Hundred and Four also controlled the senate, the generals, and the *suffetes* or *shophets*. The *shophets* were civic leaders. The name is Semitic in origin, as is the concept. Like the consuls of Rome, there were two annually elected *shophets* who acted as judges and senate presidents. They also brought issues before the Popular Assembly. Eventually, the term was used more broadly, as there were *shophets* in various locations around the Carthaginian Empire.

As has been noted, the Carthaginian Empire was not the rigid, clearly defined nation that one might think of when one thinks of an empire. Carthage gave plenty of autonomy to her possessions and relied on treaties and alliances as much as full-scale conquest. Carthage does not appear to have been in the habit of leaving garrisons in cities it conquered as the Romans and Greeks did. This was both beneficial and detrimental to Carthage since it did not need to extend its people and resources across a wide area, but it also made it easier for cities to revolt. Whole regions could be lost quickly, like Sardinia and Corsica.

For many centuries, Carthage relied heavily on its navy to protect its commercial vessels and ports and to keep its various territories in check. This, of course, changed during the Punic Wars. However, its land army was just as important and was involved in as much activity as its forces on the sea. The two areas had to often work in concert, such as when troops needed to be transported or when cities were being besieged. This meant that generals needed to have supreme authority while they engaged in military actions. Carthaginian generals did not have to wait for approval from the senate before they acted as their Roman counterparts did, but they were in danger of later prosecution from the Hundred and Four if it was deemed their actions were in error. For this reason, many Carthaginian generals were executed after serious losses.

The primary problem with this system was that the Hundred and Four could act cruelly and arbitrarily, so a general had no way of knowing if his actions would be excused or if he might be put to death after a particular battle or war. By the time of the Barcids, however, thanks to support from the Popular Assembly, generals were able to escape prosecution. When they were away from Carthage, they could essentially act as monarchs in their given territories, as Hamilcar, Hasdrubal, and Hannibal did in Spain.

The army of Carthage was incredibly successful when they were commanded by a competent general. These generals were typically selected for a particular campaign or war and almost always came from elite families. Generals were generally autonomous, but the Hundred and Four or the *shophets* might order a general to call a truce or sue for peace. Some families in Carthage also had their own private armies, which they could call upon for overseas operations. Thus, an army could have two or even three different commanders, a situation that caused many difficulties. Due to the pressure of command and the possibility of harsh punishment, many unsuccessful commanders committed suicide rather than face judgment back in Carthage. However, they could still face punishment after death. For instance, the Hundred and Four crucified the corpse of general Mago in 344 BCE.

The Carthaginian army consisted of heavy armored infantry drawn from the citizenry. They numbered 2,500 to 3,000 and were known for their white shields. They were called the Sacred Band. Infantry and cavalry units were also pulled from allies, notably the Libyans and Iberians. They were paid for their services but might not have been considered mercenaries. Additionally, Carthage employed what is typically considered mercenaries, that is, soldiers for hire. Mercenaries came from all corners of the empire and beyond, such as Gaul, Iberia, Greece, Sardinia, and Tunisia, to name a few. The Carthaginians also employed the Numidian cavalry, whose men carried small shields and threw poisoned darts. The Numidians would, of course, play a crucial role in the lead-up to the Third Punic War when they opposed Carthage. The Carthaginians also had a unit of Egyptian-Libyan women who rode chariots into battle.

The Carthaginians often used the armor of their fallen enemies. After the Sicilian Wars, they commonly used bronze Corinthian helmets and heavy hoplite armor. Their shields were typically circular, though Celtic soldiers had rectangular oak shields. Shields were often decorated with designs from the Punic religion or, in the case of Hasdrubal Barca, self-portraits. Hannibal wore gilded bronze-scaled armor that had belonged to Hamilcar, his father. Soldiers typically carried straight or curved blades with a dagger for backup. The armor and weapons varied greatly due to the many different origins of the units that made up the Carthaginian army.

There were archers, but they were used less than in other contemporary armies. However, there were typically archers on top of the war elephants. There were slingers as well, with the most famous being the Balearic slingers, who used almond-shaped lead shot. The Punic army also used catapults and crossbows.

The Carthaginians were perhaps most famous for their use of war elephants. These massive creatures were used as much for their psychological effect as their importance on the battlefield. Elephants were trained to charge, but they could be unwieldy. In many instances, they turned and trampled the men in their own army rather than the enemy. They were often covered in armor, with spears attached to their trunks. The elephants used were native to North Africa and are now extinct. They were not large enough to carry any structure on their backs but instead had a rider and a bowman or javelin thrower. The elephants were typically placed in front of the infantry when battle lines were formed.

The Carthaginian army was used to great effect by Hannibal in his Spanish and Italian campaigns. He did not rely too heavily on the war elephants but instead used his cavalry to outflank his enemy. He was also a master of the ambush and was able to catch the Romans by surprise on various occasions and use this to his advantage. Hannibal appears to have planned out every detail and communicated his plans to all parts of his army so that they could work together as one unit and exploit the weaknesses of his enemy.

Despite the arguments of Greek and Roman historians, the Carthaginian army was in no way inferior due to their use of mercenaries or because of the natural disposition of the Carthaginians themselves. Hannibal was not an aberration but the product of a system designed to maintain one of the greatest powers in the western Mediterranean.

Chapter Ten: Society, Economy, and Religion

The Carthaginian society was born, first and foremost, from its Phoenician origin. The language they spoke was derived from Phoenician, the gods they prayed to were, at first, Phoenician gods, and their commerce was built around the Phoenician model. The Phoenician cities of the Levant were primarily maritime cultures. Carthage seems to have adopted that in many ways, but the Carthaginians did venture into their own hinterland for territory and did not rely on a network of ports from which to trade. They were expansionists to a large degree, which was nothing particularly unique in the time and place they lived. They were not, as some have suggested, solely interested in commerce and currency. The Carthaginians had very keen concepts of duty, honor, and loyalty.

The Romans might have thought the idea of Punic loyalty was a joke, but the Carthaginians were not in any way more scheming or two-faced than the Romans themselves. It was the Romans, after all, who pretended to consider peace during the Third Punic War when they had already sent an army to raze Carthage to the ground. The Romans might have thought Carthaginian generals had too much power and were verging on being tyrants, but a few generations after Carthage was destroyed, Rome would be rocked by a civil war caused by the dictator-for-life Julius Caesar.

Still, it is true that the Carthaginians exploited native populations for their own gain, but this was just as true for every one of their neighbors. Syracuse might have felt that Carthage had no claim to Sicily, but Syracuse was founded and populated by the Greeks. The indigenous people of Sicily suffered at the hands of both of these powers. Every nation of the ancient Mediterranean practiced slavery, and Carthage was certainly no exception.

Depiction of Baal Hammon.
https://commons.wikimedia.org/wiki/File:Bardo_Baal_Thinissut.jpg

The chief gods of Carthage were Baal Hammon and his consort Tanit. Baal Hammon was a weather god and the god of fertility. He was the chief of the gods and was often associated with the Greek Cronus and Roman Saturn. Many parents sacrificed their children to Baal Hammon.

He was derived from the Phoenician god Baal, hence his first name, while his last name remains something of a mystery. He became the primary god of Carthage after the link between Carthage and Tyre ended.

Tanit was closely associated with the Phoenician goddess Astarte and was considered the co-chief god along with Baal

Hammon. She was a war goddess, virginal unmarried mother, and nurse. At times, she was associated with the Roman Juno as a goddess named *Dea Caelestis*. She was sometimes associated with the crescent moon. In art, she was often depicted naked and riding a lion or with a lion's head. She was also associated with the dove, the palm tree, and the rose.

The largest site yet discovered of evidence of Carthaginian child sacrifice was a tophet near the temple of Tanit, the Tophet of Salammbo. However, the remains found at the tophet indicate children of very young ages. Some scholars have suggested this is evidence that it was a site for the burial of children who died of natural causes, not child sacrifice.

The Carthaginians also worshiped the Phoenician god of healing, Eshmun, who was associated primarily with the Levantine city of Sidon. Their chief god before the break with Tyre was Melqart, who they still worshiped afterward. Melqart was the primary god of Tyre, so he became popular all around the Mediterranean world. He was often associated with Heracles, also called Hercules, and had worshippers in Sicily, Sardinia, and Spain.

Hannibal was a faithful follower of the cult of Melqart. He believed he had a vision sent to him by the god before he set out on his journey through the Alps. He dreamed of a giant serpent causing destruction along its path and was told this was the foretold destruction of Italy.

The Phoenician goddess Astarte was also popular. She was closely associated with Ishtar, a Mesopotamian goddess. She was associated with war, sex, royal power, healing, and hunting. She was often shown as a combatant on horseback or on the prow of a ship extending her arm forward; thus, she was most likely the inspiration for ship figureheads.

A thunder god, also associated with plague, war, and protection, was worshiped in Carthage. His name was Resheph. Resheph was a very old god who is believed to have made his way from Egypt to Canaan to Phoenicia and finally to Carthage. The Carthaginians also worshiped an ancient Mesopotamian sun god named Utu, who provided justice and protection to travelers. Carthage adopted the Greek goddesses Demeter and Persephone in the 4th century BCE. They worshiped many Egyptian gods, such as Bes, Bastet, Isis, Osiris, and Ra. In Sardinia, they worshiped a deity named Sid Babi, who was believed to be the son of Melqart.

Carthage ruled over an eclectic empire, and Carthaginian society reflected this. Dominating everything was the elite Carthaginian class; some families could likely trace their heritage back to the beginning of the city or to the mother city, Tyre. All the important political and religious positions were held by this group. But they only represented a small portion of the Carthaginian population. Carthage was home to skilled artisans, wealthy merchants, laborers, mercenaries, and slaves. In every city under Carthaginian control, there would have been various populations of foreigners who were part of the commercial and cultural exchange happening in the western Mediterranean. At its peak, the city of Carthage was home to 400,000 people. It was a cosmopolitan city that blended old, new, rich, and poor.

However, most people only wanted to know about the riches the city held. Roman writers called it the richest city in the world, and this might have been true for a time. Precious metals, art, jewels, glass, ivory, and alabaster were constantly coming in and out of Carthage's large harbors. The elite were, above all else, amazingly wealthy. In fact, land ownership was not required to be counted among the aristocrats; all that one needed was to be extremely wealthy. Therefore, it is possible that enterprising individuals could make use of the vibrant markets in Carthage and make themselves rich and then turn that into political power. Aristotle thought the preoccupation with wealth was unhealthy.

The aristocrats also had control of religious life in Carthage. The head of the priests was also a member of the Senate and was on the Council of the Hundred and Four. That incredibly powerful position could only be held by someone with extensive wealth and the backing of other aristocratic families. However, the priestly positions were often hereditary and required an austere life.

Priests were noticeable for their shaved heads. However, due to the destruction of Carthage in 146 BCE, we do not know what the initiation rituals were for priests or if they served for life. There were female priests as well, but very little is known about them.

Priests may have had a hand in education or maintaining the libraries of Carthage, but this is speculation.

Citizens were exclusively males, and they could participate in the Popular Assembly, which was relatively powerless until the rise of the Barcids. However, political positions were not paid in Carthage, so there is the question of who could afford to engage in politics and forgo a trade. The citizens were separated into various groups, possibly families or if they fought together in a battle. There were certainly powerful trade guilds in the city as well. These groups held regular banquets, where they discussed important matters and enjoyed each other's company. Unlike other ancient societies, the Carthaginians were not expected to perform military service, save the members of the Sacred Band.

Despite a few previously mentioned instances, the Carthaginians did not, as a rule, resort to rebellion very often. There are many theories for this. It seems most likely that because Carthage remained relatively prosperous for much of its history, the general public never felt particularly motivated to challenge the oligarchy that ruled them. Citizens might not even have been taxed, so not much was asked of them. They were able to work and earn enough to live fairly comfortably, so they never felt it was necessary to overthrow the government that was protecting them. Also, it has been suggested that because political appointments were unpaid and because military service was not compulsory, Carthaginians might not have really known how to effect change even if they wanted to. Of course, this is, again, speculation. Because we lack records of Carthaginian history written by the citizens' own hands, we do not know the exact nature of the struggles the citizenry might have faced.

Carthage was certainly a male-dominated society. Women could not be citizens, and inscriptions that refer to women typically mention her in relation to her father or husband. Women lacked not only a voice in Carthaginian history but also names.

Carthage was home to many artisans, metal workers, potters, and glass makers. The raw materials might have come from various places in the empire, but they were shaped and molded within the walls of the capital city. The artisans made weapons, statues, and pillars. They made cloth and dyed it the famous purple. Many workers lived in the same neighborhood, in a potter's district, or in a metal workers' conclave. Workshops used citizen labor and slaves. Carthage was famous for the wide-eyed, grinning masks it produced.

Just as important were the sailors, dockworkers, and porters who labored in the various harbors and on board the massive fleets of commercial vessels that traveled from port to port within the empire and beyond. There were cooks, scribes, shopkeepers, doctors, and fishermen in every corner of the Carthaginian Empire. There were also interpreters who could help foreigners and Punic speakers conduct business.

Slaves were a normal part of Carthaginian society. They were used in the countryside and in the city for menial and important tasks; they even served in the navy during the Second Punic War. Citizens could not become slaves, as was the case in Rome. But slaves could become free, though they most likely never enjoyed the benefits of being a citizen. Slaves had general autonomy and ran businesses for their masters. Carthaginian inscriptions indicate that slaves could accumulate their own wealth, as some inscriptions were paid for by slaves. At the end of the Third Punic War, slaves were given their freedom to help protect the doomed city.

Perhaps Carthage's greatest success was its trade. Like their Phoenician forefathers, the Carthaginians were particularly focused on establishing trade networks around the Mediterranean to accumulate wealth. They were renowned for their ability to sell anything to anyone at a price that made them a profit. The location of Carthage was most likely picked because of its excellent harbor and the fact that it lay on two incredibly important trade routes. One route went from Spain to the Levant, and the other went from North Africa to Sicily and Italy. Being in such a spot meant that Carthage was perhaps destined for prosperity, but the Carthaginians did not rest on that alone. From the city's founding, they embarked on trading expeditions all around the Mediterranean and even out into the Atlantic. They established trade routes from North Africa to Sardinia, Spain, Corsica, Malta, Cyprus, and Sicily.

Due to the expedition down the West African coast by Hanno the Navigator, Carthage may have traded with indigenous people in western Africa and possibly as far as Britain if the story of Himilco can be believed. These territories provided Carthage with a multitude of important goods, none more important than silver, which was the standard currency of ancient times. Carthage followed what would become the standard of trade to our present day. The Carthaginians were able to buy things like metals at very low rates, ship them somewhere that had no such natural resources, and sell them at a remarkable profit. They continued this strategy for their entire history. It worked exceptionally well.

   Carthage formed colonies where these raw materials were being extracted. The colony's sole purpose was to ensure that the flow of the commodities continued unabated. Rebellions and revolts disrupted the flow, as did wars with outside enemies. This is perhaps why Carthage was quicker to resolve issues with diplomacy and agreed to pay fines regardless of whether the outcome was just since it was more important that trade continued.

   The Carthaginians didn't just explore the sea; they are also known to have established trade routes across the Sahara as well. They also traded with Greece, Egypt, Hellenistic kingdoms, and Rome. Was there a better place to sell silver and bronze than in places like Greece that relied on silver and bronze but had very little in their own country? The Carthaginians turned up everywhere. They traded in markets in Athens, Rome, Delos, Rhodes, and Syracuse. They sold their goods in Tyre, Sidon, and Byblos, becoming the child who beat their parent at their own game.

   Carthaginian coins are of particular interest to scholars since they are one of the few artifacts of Carthage that remain in existence. During good times, Carthaginian coins were made of gold, silver, electrum (a combination of gold and silver), and bronze. During hard times, coins were made of bronze, though it seems soldiers were always paid in bronze. It also seems that trade was not just conducted by private individuals but also by the state. The powerful Carthaginian navy was used to protect commercial vessels and trading routes. If the navy found a foreign ship in what was believed to be exclusive Carthaginian waters, that ship was sunk. Pirates were dealt with in the same way.

The Carthaginians most likely traded a wide variety of items. This was used to comic effect in a Greek play, in which a Carthaginian character, Hanno, is said to have a cargo of pipes, shoe straps, and panthers. The Carthaginians certainly traded in gold, tin, silver, copper, lead, iron, wool, amber, ivory, and incense. They also traded slaves. They were known for their luxury items like fine art, textiles, furniture, carpets, and cushions. They also traded in olives, olive oil, salted fish, wine, pomegranates, nuts, herbs, and spices. The problem, of course, was competition. Due to competition, they lost the war in Sicily and then the Punic Wars, which cost them everything.

Conclusion

The story of Carthage is truly one about reaching great heights only to fall from that lofty perch. However, its complete destruction by Rome does not discount its domination of the western Mediterranean for centuries.

Its story is perhaps best exemplified by the most famous Carthaginian of all: Hannibal Barca. Hannibal, who was intelligent and proud, took on tasks that seemed impossible, but he accomplished them and continued to reap victories. However, Hannibal finally met Scipio and lost everything his family had built and everything Carthage had achieved through long years of struggle and perseverance in a single battle. It is what is written on every gravestone and every clock face: all things come to an end. And just as Rome brought the end of Carthage, it, too, was heading toward its own demise.

Though the story of Carthage may have ended poorly for anyone who called themselves a Carthaginian, and though that history has been obscured almost beyond understanding, there is still greatness that shines through. There is still, somewhere in the mists of time, a great city of traders, artists, aristocrats, and priests, and there are still harbors filled with ships heading off into the dark sea destined to make a fortune.

Here's another book by Enthralling History that you might like

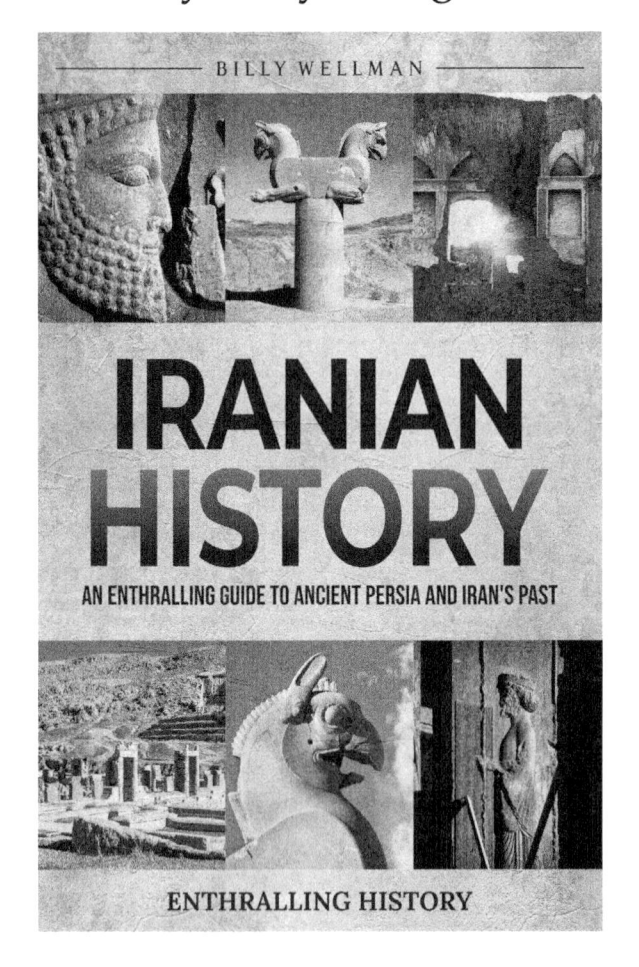

Free limited time bonus

Stop for a moment. We have a free bonus set up for you. The problem is this: we forget 90% of everything that we read after 7 days. Crazy fact, right? Here's the solution: we've created a printable, 1-page pdf summary for this book that you're reading now. All you have to do to get your free pdf summary is to go to the following website:

https://livetolearn.lpages.co/enthrallinghistory/

Once you do, it will be intuitive. Enjoy, and thank you!

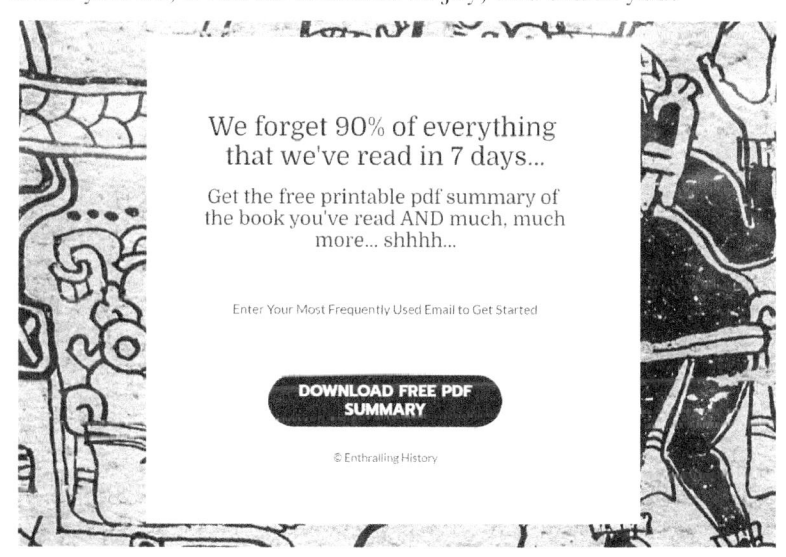

Works Cited

Battle of Ticinus, November 218 BC, 31 March 2002, http://www.historyofwar.org/articles/battles_ticinus.html. Accessed 22 November 2022.

Battle of Cannae, https://www.cs.mcgill.ca/~rwest/wikispeedia/wpcd/wp/b/Battle_of_Cannae.htm. Accessed 23 November 2022.

"Ancient Carthage | World Civilization." *Lumen Learning*, https://courses.lumenlearning.com/suny-hccc-worldcivilization/chapter/ancient-carthage/. Accessed 13 November 2022.

"Ancient Tyre." *World Monuments Fund*, https://www.wmf.org/project/ancient-tyre. Accessed 4 November 2022.

Cartwright, Mark. "Carthaginian Society." *World History Encyclopedia*, 16 June 2016, https://www.worldhistory.org/article/908/carthaginian-society/. Accessed 25 November 2022.

Cartwright, Mark, and Alexander van Loon. "Carthaginian Army." *World History Encyclopedia*, 8 June 2016, https://www.worldhistory.org/Carthaginian_Army/. Accessed 25 November 2022.

Corinne, Bonnet. "Religion, Phoenician and Punic." *Oxford Classical Dictionary*, Oxford University, 30 05 2020, oxfordre.com/classics. Accessed 3 11 2022.

Cremin, Aedeen, editor. *The World Encyclopedia of Archaeology: The World's Most Significant Sites and Cultural Treasures.* Firefly Books, 2007.

"The First Punic War." *Dickinson College Commentaries,* https://dcc.dickinson.edu/nepos-hannibal/first-punic-war. Accessed 18 November 2022.

Herodotus. *The Landmark Herodotus: The Histories.* Edited by Robert B. Strassler, translated by Andrea L. Purvis, Knopf Doubleday Publishing Group, 2009.

Hunt, Patrick, and E. Badian. "Battle of the Trebbia River | Roman-Carthaginian history." *Encyclopedia Britannica,* https://www.britannica.com/event/Battle-of-the-Trebbia-River. Accessed 22 November 2022.

Justinus, Marcus Junianus, and Justin. *Epitome of the Philippic History of Pompeius Trogus.* Edited by R. Develin, translated by J. C. Yardley, Scholars Press, 1994.

Liver, J. "The Chronology of Tyre at the Beginning of the First Millennium B.C." *Israel Exploration Journal,* vol. 3, no. 2, 1953, pp. 113-120. *JSTOR,* http://www.jstor.org/stable/27924517. Accessed 4 11 2022.

Merideth, C. "Northwestern Iberian Tin Mining from Bronze Age to Modern Times: an overview." *Archive ouverte HAL,* 21 March 2019, https://hal.archives-ouvertes.fr/hal-02024038/document. Accessed 13 November 2022.

Miles, Richard. *Carthage Must Be Destroyed: The Rise and Fall of an Ancient Civilization.* Penguin Publishing Group, 2012.

Paton, W. R., translator. *The Complete Histories of Polybius.* Digireads.com, 2009.

"Phoenix | Facts, Information, and Mythology." *Encyclopedia Mythica,* 3 March 1997, https://pantheon.org/articles/p/phoenix2.html. Accessed 3 November 2022.

"Punic." *U-M Library Digital Collections,* https://quod.lib.umich.edu/d/did/did2222.0003.974/--punic?rgn=main;view=fulltext;q1=Paul+Henri+Dietrich%2C+baron+d++Holbach. Accessed 8 November 2022.

Quinn, Josephine. *In Search of the Phoenicians.* Princeton University Press, 2019.

Sasson, Jack M. "The Phoenicians (1500–300 B.C.) | Essay | The Metropolitan Museum of Art | Heilbrunn Timeline of Art History." *Metropolitan Museum of Art,* https://www.metmuseum.org/toah/hd/phoe/hd_phoe.htm. Accessed 2 November 2022.

Sullivan, Richard E. "Hieron II | tyrant and king of Syracuse." *Encyclopedia Britannica*, https://www.britannica.com/biography/Hieron-II. Accessed 18 November 2022.

Thucydides. *The Landmark Thucydides: A Comprehensive Guide to the Peloponnesian War.* Edited by Richard Crawley and Robert B. Strassler, translated by Victor Davis Hanson and Richard Crawley, Free Press, 1998.

Torr, Cecil. "The Harbours of Carthage." *The Classical Review*, vol. 5, no. 6, 1891, pp. 280-284. *JSTOR*, http://www.jstor.org/stable/693421. Accessed 11 11 2022.

Urbanus, Jason. "Masters of the Ancient Mediterranean." *Archaeology*, vol. 69, no. 3, 2016, pp. 38-43. *JSTOR*, http://www.jstor.org/stable/43825141. Accessed 07 11 2022.

Wolters, Edward J. "Carthage and Its People." *The Classical Journal*, vol. 47, no. 5, 1952, pp. 191-204. *JSTOR*, http://www.jstor.org/stable/3293326. Accessed 7 11 2022.

Printed in Great Britain
by Amazon